MEASURING COMMUNITY INDICATORS

Applied Social Research Methods Series
Volume 45

APPLIED SOCIAL RESEARCH METHODS SERIES

Series Editors
LEONARD BICKMAN, Peabody College, Vanderbilt University, Nashville
DEBRA J. ROG, Vanderbilt University, Washington, DC

Other volumes in this series are listed at the end of the book

MEASURING COMMUNITY INDICATORS

A Systems Approach to Drug and Alcohol Problems

Paul J. Gruenewald
Andrew J. Treno
Gail Taff
Michael Klitzner

Applied Social Research Methods Series
Volume 45

SAGE Publications
International Educational and Professional Publisher
Thousand Oaks London New Delhi

Do not copy, quote, or paraphrase without permission of the first author.

Research and preparation for this paper were supported by the Center for Substance Abuse Prevention (CSAP) and the National Institute on Alcohol Abuse and Alcoholism (NIAAA) under grant #AA09146 and by the Robert Wood Johnson Foundation.

For information address:

SAGE Publications, Inc.
2455 Teller Road
Thousand Oaks, California 91320
e-mail: order@sagepub.com

SAGE Publications Ltd.
6 Bonhill Street
London EC2A 4PU
United Kingdom

SAGE Publications India Pvt. Ltd.
M-32 Market
Greater Kailash I
New Delhi 110 048 India

Printed in the United States of America

Library of Congress Cataloging-in-Publication Data

Measuring community indicators : a systems approach to drug and
    alcohol problems / Paul J. Gruenewald . . . [et al.]
        p. cm. — (Applied social research methods ; vol. 45)
    Includes bibliographical references and index.
    ISBN 0-7619-0684-3 (acid-free paper). — ISBN 0-7619-0685-1
(pbk.: acid-free paper)
    1. Substance abuse—United States—Statistics. 2. Substance
abuse—United States—Statistical methods. 3. Social indicators—
United States. I. Gruenewald, Paul J. II. Series: Applied social
research methods series ; v. 45.
HV4999.2.M43   1997
362.29'12'0973—dc20   96-35647

This book is printed on acid-free paper.

97 98 99 00 01 10 9 8 7 6 5 4 3 2 1

Production Editor: LaVonne Taylor
Typesetter: Rebecca Evans

Contents

Introduction

Lately, there has been an increased awareness of the importance of monitoring drug and alcohol use patterns and related problems at the local or community level. This increased awareness has arisen for a number of related reasons. First, there has been a general recognition that the solutions to drug and alcohol problems are best developed while taking into account local community-level conditions. Second, prevention, treatment, and enforcement in the areas of alcohol and other drugs increasingly have been seen as local responsibilities. Third, the funding of local community coalitions and agencies to address these problems, with a corresponding shift in administrative and budgetary authority, has provided a financial basis for this development. This trend will likely continue given the current trend toward block grants.

Because of the shift of funding and administrative authority to the local level, communities have never been in a better position to determine the course of local alcohol and drug prevention efforts. Unfortunately, relatively little attention has been directed to the development of a methodology for community monitoring of the problems communities are ostensibly to solve. As a result, practitioners and researchers in the alcohol and other drug studies field have relied on indicators of geographically specific alcohol use and related problems that, although sensible from the standpoint of face validity, remain untested. Moreover, the gap between the obvious effects of alcohol and other drug use as reflected in costs to local communities, our recognition of these issues as local problems, and our ability to estimate levels of that use with confidence are exacerbated by the fact that, at least for the foreseeable future, fewer national resources will be available to address alcohol and other drug problems. Subsequently, the need to develop rigorously defined valid and reliable monitoring tools linked to coherent theoretical frameworks in the interest of determining "what works" has become imperative. Our goal is to address this gap in the community indicators field and thus to provide communities and researchers assisting them with needed analytic and practical tools.

Our plan is as follows. First, we present the case for the collection of local community indicator data (Chapter 1). We argue that although highly aggregated national data perform a number of important research and policy functions, their purpose is largely distinct from that served by community-level data collection. In particular, we note that highly aggregated data are of questionable use to local policy-oriented officials. Second, we present a theoretical perspective, developed from community systems theory, that guides and informs the practical strategies outlined in the text (Chapter 2). We contrast this perspective with the public health model and the more traditional medical model that preceded it. In particular, we examine the character of community systems and discuss the implications of this character for community monitoring and indicator collection. Third, we discuss the current state of systems theory in the social sciences and we present, as an extended illustration of this perspective, a computer simulation model of drug and alcohol use (Chapter 3). Fourth, we present a discussion and evaluation of a number of such community indicators (Chapter 4). In particular, we focus on the limitations of the naive or exclusive use of each of these. Fifth, we discuss the potential role played by community surveys (Chapter 5) both in filling in the gaps in available data and as a check on "official statistics" that, because they are produced by the community systems they are designed to monitor, may reflect changes in community systems other than systems they are intended to monitor (e.g., decreases in drug arrests necessitated by cutbacks in police department budgets). As we argue, given the conditions under which community indicators are produced, they are most appropriately used in concert with data collected by other means. Sixth, we present a discussion of practical techniques (Chapter 6) necessary for the primary collection of community indicator data (e.g., geographic mapping, systems of community data acquisition, and community contact maintenance). The primary collection of community-level indicator data involves the meticulous application of fairly recently developed and not universally applied techniques and methods.

Chapters 1 through 6 cover a large amount of theoretical, empirical, and conceptual territory in fields relevant to the study of alcohol and drug problems. Thorough examinations of these problems requires a broad, interdisciplinary perspective that draws on the conceptual foundations of psychological, social-psychological, sociological, political, and economic thought, and methodological advances in the analysis of complex systems in macrosociology, econometrics, and evaluation re-search. In view of this interdisciplinary perspective, the broadest goal of this monograph is to acquaint individual researchers—often pursuing difficult issues with deliberate myopic intent—with the broader com-plexities of the issues at hand. To the extent that the reader becomes acquainted with the breadth and complexity of the conceptualization and measurement of community alcohol and drug problems, we will have accomplished this goal.

A caveat should be issued at this point. No single document can address all the areas of potential interest to community indicators researchers. For practical purposes, we have left a number of such areas uncovered. First, because our intention is to provide a guide in evaluat-ing the various community indicators and suggesting procedures for locating them from individual communities, we have avoided providing a compilation of secondary sources. A number of such compilations are available. One of the most impressive such compilations is *How Do We Know We Are Making A Difference: A Community Substance Abuse Indicators Handbook* (Join Together, 1995). This document provides addresses, telephone and fax numbers, and contact persons for federal, state, and local agencies responsible for compiling statistics on the use of alcohol and other drugs, crime, child abuse, education, and health. Addi-tionally, it contains information for obtaining data through computer bulletin boards and other electronic media. Last, we have avoided the area of qualitative measures (e.g., ethnography, unobtrusive measures, and the like). We have done this for a number of reasons. First, this monograph emerged out of an experience and tradition of collecting quantitative measures. Rather than stray from that experience and tra-dition in the hope of comprehensiveness, we have chosen to present a focused, if limited, subject matter. Second, and perhaps more important, the use of qualitative measures in monitoring drug and alcohol usage is a topic worthy of separate consideration. The norms guiding such an endeavor remain to be defined and are beyond the scope of this book.

This book is targeted toward a rather diverse audience and is intended to serve multiple purposes. First, it is aimed at students interested in learning more about issues associated with the assessment of commu-nity indicators of drug and alcohol use patterns and related problems. Second, it is aimed at community activists and practitioners who des-perately need assistance in understanding the dynamics underlying alcohol and other drug use in their communities. In the interest of

serving the needs of these two audiences, we have attempted to eliminate as much jargon as possible. Obviously, our desire to make this work
accessible had to compete with the need to produce a document for a
more technically trained audience. Third, it is aimed at researchers in
alcohol and other drug-related fields who are interested in exploring this
rather understudied area from a systems point of view.

1

Why Community Indicators?

As a preface to discussion of our conceptualization of a systems perspective of community indicators collection and analysis, it is necessary to compare national and local data sources and pose the legitimate question of why it is necessary to collect local data when highly aggregated national data may suffice. In our view, national alcohol and other drugs (AOD) data and similar local data serve fundamentally different purposes. Clearly, it is important to consider broad national trends in drug and alcohol use prior to undertaking individual community studies. First, these trends provide the clearest and most concise statement of the AOD problem. Second, they provide a benchmark against which individual community needs may be assessed. Third, they give some sense of the national culture from which individual community patterns of alcohol and drug use are derived. Yet, based on our review of national data, these do not suffice to meet the needs of local policymakers.

Costs of Alcohol Use

That the direct and indirect costs of alcohol use at the national level are substantial remains beyond question. Some 47% of all fatal traffic crashes, the primary cause of accidental death in the United States, are estimated to be alcohol related (Evans, 1990; 18.2 per 100,000, Aitken & Zobeck, 1985). Seventy to eighty-nine percent of single vehicle nighttime fatal crashes (crashes involving a single motor vehicle between the hours of 12:00 pm and 3:00 am, Zador, Lund, Fields, & Weinberg, 1988) are considered by experts to involve alcohol. Alcohol use is related to the incidence of the second, third, and fourth leading causes of accidental death in the United States—falls, drownings, and burns (11 per 100,000, Saltz, Gruenewald, & Hennessy, 1992), and deaths due to the direct physiological consequences of alcohol use (4.4 per 100,000 alcohol-related deaths due to cirrhosis, Williams, Grant, Stinson, Zobeck, Aitken, & Noble, 1988).

1

Moreover, direct morbidity and mortality accounts for only a proportion of the total economic costs to society of alcohol abuse. Loss of productivity at work and treatment for alcohol abuse and related problems are also major drains on America's assets. Estimates of costs to insurance companies for treatment of an alcoholic worker average about $5,000 per patient (Holder & Blose, 1991), overall health care costs are 100% higher in families with alcoholic members than without (Holder, Lennox, & Blose, 1992), and treatment costs for alcohol problems exceed $1.2 billion per year from federal, state, local, and private sources (Department of Health and Human Services, 1992).

Additional social and economic costs related to alcohol use relate to efforts at the enforcement of alcohol laws (e.g., minimum drinking age laws and laws related to drunkenness and drunk driving). Six hundred twenty-four thousand arrests were made in 1991 for violations of alcohol control laws (largely sales to minors), 881,000 arrests were made for public drunkenness (Department of Justice, 1992), and 1.8 million arrests were made for driving under the influence of alcohol (1 out of every 92 licensed drivers, National Highway Traffic Safety Administration, 1992). In aggregate, alcohol-related arrests accounted for 23% of all arrests reported in the United States in 1991, reflecting a capitated rate of 1,263 arrests per 100,000 population.

Costs of Illicit Drug Use

The social and economic consequences of the use of illicit drugs in the United States are equally alarming. Moreover, illicit substance use poses additional costs associated with police enforcement at municipal, county, state, federal, and international levels. Thus the costs of enforcing laws directed at the suppression of the illegal drug trade must be added to the social and economic costs of use itself. For example, there were 1 million arrests for drug abuse violations in 1991 (Department of Justice, 1992), of which 33.4% were for sales and/or manufacturing of illegal substances. More than 9,000 arrests were made and $53 million in assets were seized in arrests made for the illegal production of marijuana (Drug Enforcement Administration, 1992). United States support of international drug interdiction, a focus of supply-side reduction efforts during the late 1980s (Reuter, 1992), was $307 million in fiscal year 1990, with a planned budget of $612 million in 1992 (Office of National Drug Control Policy, 1991). The U.S. Customs Service reports having seized 174,000 pounds of heroin, cocaine, and opium; 465,000 pounds of marijuana and hashish; and 3 million doses of other drugs, barbiturates, and LSD in 1991 (Department of Treasury, 1991).

The influence of illegal drug use on the health care system is also substantial. There were 371,000 drug abuse-related emergency room episodes in 1990 (Department of Health and Human Services, 1991). Deaths due to cocaine or opiate poisoning occurred at a rate of .35 per 100,000 people in 1987, rising 278% over the period from the late 1970s to the mid-1980s (Baker, O'Neill, Ginsburg, & Li, 1992). Deaths due to opiate poisoning occurred at a rate of .25 per 100,000 people in 1987, rising some 143% over the same period of time. In response, federal, state, local, and private funding sources spent more than $1.2 billion in 1991 on prevention and treatment programs aimed at reducing drug problems (Department of Health and Human Services, 1992). When prevention and treatment of alcohol problems are also considered, this figure rises to $4.1 billion. More than 2,400 active community coalitions, comprising some 8,000 individuals, exist in the United States and its territories with the expressed purpose of preventing alcohol and drug problems (Rosenbloom, Dawkins, & Hingson, 1992).

From federal sources alone, the overall cost of enforcement, prevention, treatment, and research into alcohol and drug abuse was $12 billion in 1992 (Executive Office of the President, 1992), amounting to a cost to each citizen of $48 per year. Taking into account the complete human costs due to alcohol and drug use and abuse at the federal, state, and local levels (including indirect economic costs due to lost productivity), the total costs of alcohol- and drug-related problems were estimated to be $114 billion in 1985 and $144 billion in 1988 (Rice, Kelman, Miller, & Dunmeyer, 1990), a cost to each citizen of from $456 to $576 per year.

What Have We Purchased?

Despite the billions of dollars spent by federal, state, and local governments on efforts to minimize drug and alcohol problems among adults and youth in the United States, the demand for drugs and alcohol continues. In a 1993 national survey of high school seniors, 78% reported using alcohol sometime in the past 12 months, 26% reported using marijuana, 8% stimulants, 7% inhalants, 7% hallucinogens, 3% sedatives and tranquilizers, and 4% cocaine (Johnston, O'Malley, & Bachman, 1994). In a recent national household survey, 71% of individuals 18 years of age and older reported using alcohol in the past year, 12% reported using marijuana, and 3% reported using cocaine (National Institute on Drug Abuse, 1991).

Although there was some decline in reported alcohol, marijuana, and cocaine use among young people from 1979 to 1993 (Johnston, O'Malley,

& Bachman, 1992, 1993), this decline was countered by an increase in reported adult use of these substances over the same period (National Institute on Drug Abuse, 1991). These changes appear related to long-term alterations in usage patterns dating back to 1972. During this time, all forms of drug use increased to a peak in 1979, then subsequently decreased, with the decreases appearing more gradually among older rather than younger individuals. By 1990, levels of alcohol, marijuana, and cocaine use still exceeded those observed among adults 26 years and older in the early 1970s. Alcohol and cocaine use increased and marijuana use decreased among adults 18 to 25 years, and alcohol and marijuana use decreased, whereas cocaine use increased for youth 12 to 17 years of age (past year use, National Institute on Drug Abuse, 1991).[1] Thus, even at the national level, changes in drug use patterns appear quite complicated and differ by age cohort and substance.

To what extent can community-level patterns of alcohol and drug use and resulting problems be viewed as a simple reflection of broader national trends? Are communities merely microcosms of the larger national aggregate? To answer these questions, we must consider the diversity that characterizes community AOD experiences.

DIFFERENCES IN USE PATTERNS
AT THE COMMUNITY LEVEL

The National Institute on Drug Abuse's (NIDA) National Household Survey has recently been expanded to allow comparisons of drug use patterns among six large urban environments and between these urban areas and the nation as a whole. In aggregate, rates of self-reported use in the urban areas are quite similar to those observed at the national level (Hughes, 1992). Differences among the urban areas are also sometimes dramatic, however. For example, the reported rate of past-month illicit drug use was 57% greater in Los Angeles than in Miami. Moreover, less direct sources of data on illegal drug use in urban areas suggest that the abuse of illegal drugs may be climbing rapidly in some inner-city environments, perhaps driven by increasing frequencies of use by current users rather than the recruitment of new users (Johnson, Williams, Dei, & Sanabria, 1990). The NIDA's Drug Abuse Warning Network (DAWN) operates in nine metropolitan areas to measure numbers of admissions to emergency rooms following the use of any illegal drug. The number of admissions following cocaine use increased by 421%

from 1984 to 1988 (National Institute on Drug Abuse, 1989). Over the same period, the number of admissions to emergency rooms following the combined use of cocaine and heroin ("speedballing") increased 180%. Thus it appears that substantial diversity characterizes communities in terms of local drug use patterns.

Drugs and Crime

If drug use differs substantially between communities, are these differences reflected in problems such as drug-related crimes? Perhaps the most obvious connections between drugs and crimes at the community level derive from the fact that the sale and distribution of illegal drugs is clearly a lucrative trade in many urban areas. In 1986, the total value of illicit drugs on the market exceeded $100 billion (President's Commission on Organized Crime, 1986). The total value today is, no doubt, much greater. And, as noted by Johnson et al. (1990), successful dealers can clear profits of up to $100,000 per year without paying taxes. Thus, economic incentives to enter the trade in illegal drugs are great. The management of a drug dealing operation, however, requires the establishment of a system of violence and intimidation to ward off competition and to enforce anonymity of sales and sellers for protection from the police. Additionally, impoverished users, having exhausted other economic means, often resort to property and consensual crimes (theft, burglary, robbery, and prostitution) to generate the funds necessary to continue use (Hunt, 1990; Johnson et al., 1990). Thus, although the direction of causality is debated, it is certain that there are strong associations between drug use and crime. Indeed, the National Institute of Justice's (NIJ) Drug Use Forecasting system shows that in 1991, 67% of arrestees from 24 urban areas tested positive for some drug, primarily cocaine (National Institute of Justice, 1992). Furthermore, data on the extent of drug sales in cities of 100,000 people or more show that arrests for sales and possession increased by 130% from 1980 to 1989 (Federal Bureau of Investigation Uniform Crime Reports, cited in Maquire & Flanagan, 1991), with increases exceeding 500% in 15 urban communities.

How is the association between drugs and crime likely to manifest itself in community-level differences in crime? Perhaps this is most clearly demonstrated by considering the issue of community size and density. Urban areas, although not necessarily unusual for the extent to which their populations use drugs, are often the centers of a vital drug trade—a trade that attracts individuals prone to violence and intimidation. Urban areas may also attract populations of addicts who need to generate ready cash through criminal activities. Thus, crime related to drug sales and addiction might be expected to be concentrated in urban areas with high population density.

Although AOD-related crimes are not broken out by individual communities in the standard Federal Bureau of Investigation (FBI) report (FBI, 1992), available statistics show large differences in rates of drug- and alcohol-related arrests among communities of different sizes. For example, in 1991, rates of arrest for drug violations differed by a factor of 3.8 between communities having populations over 250,000 (818 per 100,000 population) versus those having populations under 10,000 (217 per 100,000). Rates of arrest for driving under the influence differed by a factor of 2.1 (462 versus 971 per 100,000), rates of arrest for liquor law violations differed by a factor of 3.3 (165 versus 551), and rates of arrest for drunkenness differed by a factor of 1.5 (360 versus 526). Taking these arrest data at face value, the size of a community is a strong determinant of the kinds of crime related to drugs and alcohol that communities experience.

National Versus Local Data

It is difficult to draw generalizations about any given community's alcohol and drug use and problems based on broad national trends indicated by highly aggregated data. For example, although national surveys indicate declining trends in use (e.g., the NIDA Household Survey), local data may suggest increasing trends (e.g., the DAWN reporting system). Moreover, data collected at the local level may reveal radically diverging trends in related problems among communities (e.g., FBI Uniform Crime Reports). Thus, we must question the relevance of national data to the practical concerns of communities interested in the prevention and treatment of local alcohol and drug problems. First, the diversity of drug use patterns and resulting problems suggests the futility of interpolating national patterns to local communities. Put in more practical terms, the fact that a given percentage of high school seniors nationally used marijuana in any given year tells local officials little about either the scope or the character of the drug problem in those schools for which they are responsible. Should scarce local resources be directed toward reducing marijuana use? Or are other drugs the problem in the community? Second, how are local officials to evaluate the relative effectiveness of their policies and activities given only national data? It is unlikely that the fruits of their efforts will be reflected in broad national trends. Third, at the national level, how are resources to be allocated to local jurisdictions? Should each community be viewed as reflecting broad national trends with resources allocated indiscriminately? Or should resources be targeted to those areas of greatest need? Clearly, the need to direct resources and policies to areas of greatest need necessitates the acquisition of locally relevant data. Unfortunately, having made the case for the acquisition and use of community-level data, we now must face a harsh reality. Although there has been an increased awareness that AOD problems are best understood in local terms with local solutions, there has not been a parallel development in community indicators acquisition or analysis techniques. As a result, community-level data are much more difficult to obtain than national-level data. Few currently available surveys or collations of archival materials focus on communities. What we do know about local patterns of use and resulting problems comes primarily from the NIDA Household Survey, the NIDA Drug Abuse Warning Network, the NIJ Drug Use Forecasting System, and the FBI Uniform Crime Reporting System. Although these are critical resources in the assessment of local community AOD problems and efforts, they do not provide sufficient information for the development of complex theoretically driven models of the sort argued in the following pages.

Given the need to collect more local data, the issue arises as to how this is best accomplished. Clearly, the collection of adequate local community epidemiological data concerning drug and alcohol use and problems requires either (1) the expansion of state and national surveys and monitoring systems to local areas, an unlikely development given recent trends toward decentralization or (2) the development of models of community alcohol and drug problems that provide a basis for the rational use of indirect indicators (e.g., arrests, appearances at emergency rooms for drug- and alcohol-related problems, admissions for drug and alcohol treatment). The goal of this monograph is to present in detail the techniques and underlying theoretical framework necessary for this latter endeavor.

SUMMARY

We began this chapter with a review of national patterns of alcohol and other drug use and related problems. We then argued that, given the variability of communities in these matters and the increasing tendency to view AOD policy as a local matter, national data, although useful in illustrating the scope and nature of alcohol and drug use in the United States, are insufficient for the development of AOD policy. To accomplish this, local data need to be collected and analyzed.

NOTE

1. This pattern of results strongly suggests an age-cohort effect in which early initiators of marijuana and alcohol use are aging out while a new cohort of cocaine users is growing up. Johnson, Williams, Dei, and Sanabria (1990) remark on the sequential development of patterns of abuse in New York city from the early 1960s to the late 1980s.

2

Community Indicators
From a Systems Perspective

In Chapter 1, we argued for the collection of indicator data on alcohol and other drug use and problems at the community level. Specifically, we argued that although national-, or even state-, level data serve particular functions, these differ from those served by community indicators monitoring. In this chapter, we outline a systems perspective that informs the techniques developed in later chapters. To provide a historical context for our discussion, it is useful to consider the history of concern with community indicators, the social indicators movement.

THE SOCIAL INDICATORS MOVEMENT

The use of archival data for the evaluation of social problems has a distinguished history in the social sciences in the United States. A focus at the national level on social problems and the collection of social indicators arose with the rise of interest in economic indicators in the 1960s (Land & Spilerman, 1975). Yet the inadequacy of social theory and the imprecision of social measurement—as compared to economic theory and measurement—led to the waning of interest in social indicators at the national level (MacRae, 1985). Although a small cottage industry in the social sciences arose in the 1970s addressing the measurement of the social health and quality of life in the United States, these efforts failed due to lack of specificity of the approach (Land & Spilerman, 1975) and irrelevance to institutional needs (Innes, 1990).

Although a number of obituaries have pronounced the death of the social indicators movement (Innes, 1990; MacRae, 1985), one cannot resist paraphrasing Mark Twain and noting that these rumors have been greatly exaggerated. To be sure, the social indicators movement (if there ever was one) suffered from overly ambitious scope, factionalization of theory and method, and a peculiar tendency to devolve into theoretically soft issues regarding "quality of life." Nevertheless, the social indicators

9

movement represented a growth spurt in the variety of approaches to the understanding and analysis of social systems from a quantitative perspective.

The key text of the social indicators movement (Land & Spilerman, 1975) touches on issues fundamental to the contemporary quantitative treatments of social problems in economics, sociology, and political science. Issues as diverse as returns from education, models of educational success, change in political ideology, social mobility, medical care utilization, the diffusion of disease, organizational change, divorce, and crime are addressed. The methods applied are as diverse as continuous and discrete dynamic modeling, comparative statistics, mathematical models of disease and population growth, and Markov chains.

With a view to the current relevance of social indicators to policymakers (Innes, 1990), and with an acknowledgment of the theoretical and technical developments of the past 30 years, it is timely to reconsider the use of social indicators for the assessment of community alcohol and drug problems. The sociopolitical issues of concern are relatively clearly delineated (e.g., crime related to alcohol and drug use, acute traumatic injuries realized as a consequence of acute use, and costs of treatment for chronic use), social and political institutions are in place that have a vested interest in dealing with these problems (e.g., judicial, educational, and health care systems), and academic research has considered the roles each institution plays in addressing alcohol and drug abuse (e.g., in criminological, prevention, education, and treatment studies). What remains to be explored is how complex community systems affect alcohol and drug problems in the real world—the setting in which the data observed by researchers and known here as community indicators are generated. Once this is accomplished, the specific techniques appropriate to the collection and analysis may be considered. In our view, the failure of the social indicators movement was twofold. First, it failed to be guided by a coherent theoretical systems perspective. Second, as a result, it failed to develop adequate data collection and analysis models.

COMMUNITY INDICATORS
AND COMMUNITY SYSTEMS

Although there is much potential ambiguity to the term, a *community* can generally be defined as a contiguous geopolitical area overseen by a common political structure with common policing and enforcement agencies and common educational and utility systems, and in which individuals are in daily physical contact for the purposes of economic and social exchange. *Subcommunities* can be defined as subregions of communities in which resident populations are segregated along socio-economic (e.g., dominant ethnic group composition, income groups) and/or geopolitical lines.

Thus, the definition of community used here is a functional one, reflecting Stoneall's (1983) *network-exchange perspective*—a view in which a community is defined by economic and social exchange, social control, participation, and support (also see Warren, 1983). This definition provides a basis for both focused community-level interventions and the development of specific community systems models (Holder, 1992). Under this definition, human organizational and institutional arrangements are sufficiently homogenous to allow reasonably precise specifications of community systems related to drug and alcohol problems.

This definition, moreover, reflects the fuzzy boundaries found in communities themselves. Communities will be more-or-less well-defined depending on geographic, economic, political, and social circumstances. For example, although the communities of Houston and Dallas, Texas, share some of the same political systems (federal and state governments), they have distinct city governments; distinct public transit, utility, and educational systems; and distinct local police departments and are separated by a large geographic region in which little contiguous community contact occurs. Thus, these two communities are quite separable. On the other hand, a community like Beverly Hills, California (a subdivision of Los Angeles County adjacent to the cities of West Hollywood, Hollywood, Los Angeles, Santa Monica, and Bel-Air) is only weakly separable from its neighbors. Beverly Hills has its own city government and police department, but shares common county, state, and federal governments with adjacent areas; shares various public transit, utility, and educational systems; and has contiguous borders with surrounding communities with which continuous economic and social contacts are maintained. Although both Houston and Beverly Hills are communities, the first is clearly more separable from surrounding communities than the second, and institutional and organizational arrangements are more homogenous. Assessments of drug and alcohol problems in Houston can be much more location specific than in Beverly Hills.

In the context of these definitions, *community systems* are composed of functional units of a community (e.g., police, fire, and public utilities) that have been formed for the purpose of accomplishing specific community-based objectives (e.g., law enforcement, fire protection, and the provision of power and water). Actors in community systems characteristically collect archival data for the purposes of tracking performance (e.g., arrests, responses to fires, units of power and water delivered). Thus, community indicators typically arise as measures of the performance of community systems and may only indirectly represent the concepts of interest in community research (e.g., rates of crime, fire danger, or utility use). The role an indicator plays in the community system that generates it and the degree to which it validly represents a concept of interest to social scientists are essential concerns when indicators are used in social research.

An Example

A common example of community indicators used in alcohol and drug research is arrests for violations of alcohol and drug control laws. Arrest records arise as part of the mechanism law enforcement agencies use to track, among other things, the performance of field officers. Arrest records reflect the objectives of the law enforcement community system—the specific and general deterrence of criminal activity. Of course, it is easy to confuse arrests with the underlying problem itself—crime. As enforcement agencies are quick to point out, however, arrests and crime are quite different things.

Consider a single crime—drunk driving (DWI). In all states in the United States, it is illegal to drive a car while alcohol intoxicated, with the criterion of intoxication varying from blood alcohol levels of .08 to .10. Police typically detect drunk driving on the basis of poor driving performance, decide whether or not to apprehend the driver of the vehicle, and decide to perform one of a variety of tests to ascertain intoxication (e.g., a field sobriety test or an alcohol breath test). An arrest results if, in the judgment of the officer, the driver fails the test. Each officer has some degree of discretion in the full range of activities leading to an arrest—from deciding whether or not to stop an individual driver through the decision concerning whether the sobriety test was passed or failed. It is estimated that the level of discretionary judgment exercised by field officers may be quite high. For example, in a recent study, some 21% of officers reported deciding not to apprehend and 42% not to arrest some drivers otherwise suspected of DWI in the year before the survey (Meyers, Heeren, & Hingson, 1989).

It is estimated that between 1 in 100 and 1 in 2,000 drunk driving events result in arrest (Beitel, Sharp, & Glauz, 1975; Hause, Voas, &

Chavez, 1982). Taking a recent conservative estimate of 1 arrest in 200 events (Perrine, Peck, & Fell, 1989), there are 199 undetected drunk driving events for each arrest. Approximately 1.8 million arrests for drunk driving occurred in 1991, providing a national rate of 360 million drunk driving violations in the same period. The obvious conclusion to be drawn from this example is that arrest data are, at best, indirect indicators of underlying criminal events. Although the presence of crime is a necessary condition for arrests to occur, numbers of arrests reflect actual criminal activity, the ability of criminals to conceal crime from police, the ability of police to detect crime, discretionary decisions of police in making arrests, and funding and person-power resource allocations within police departments. Furthermore, it is clear that patterns of policing so strongly affect arrests as to dominate fluctuations in the numbers observed (Sherman, 1992). Police crackdowns on drug sellers, for instance, have been observed to increase rates of arrest three hundred fold or more (Kleiman & Smith, 1990). Indeed, the Federal Bureau of Investigation's (FBI)'s (1992) Uniform Crime Reports warn the reader that arrests are "primarily a gauge of law enforcement's response to crime" (p. 212) and not a measure of crime itself.

To what extent do arrest data represent crime in the community? We must untangle the contributions to arrests of criminal versus enforcement activity if we are to use arrest data to measure levels of crime. Similar problems will arise in the interpretation of almost any community indicator, be it hospital admissions, school drop-out rates, median home prices, or sales of alcoholic beverages.

A Fundamental Premise

That official statistics reflect imperfectly the underlying constructs they are intended to measure is due to a simple fact: Community indicators arise in the context of community systems and are most often produced for purposes other than research. Thus, the usefulness of "undigested" indicators (e.g., raw arrest rates) in research is severely limited (Innes, 1990). This is not to say, however, that the "scientific" use of indicators is impossible, nor that the social sciences are any less scientific because their measures are, in a sense, received from society rather than generated by researchers themselves (MacRae, 1985). The scientific use of community indicators requires a more comprehensive understanding of the processes generating the observed data than is characteristically attributed to measurement in the physical sciences. Much as the estimation of a star's age from spectroscopic analysis

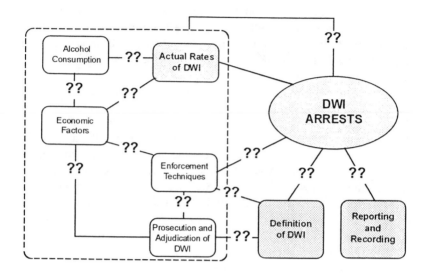

Figure 2.1. A Model of the Relationship Between Actual Rates of DWI and DWI Arrests

requires an estimate of its mass and radial velocity and a comprehensive theory of star formation, the use of most community indicators (such as arrests) requires a model of the relationship of these indicators to the object of measurement (crime).

This means that each indicator must be understood as a product of the system it is collected to analyze. Thus, increased arrests for driving while intoxicated might mean that drunk driving has increased, that an enforcement crackdown is underway, that drunk drivers have become less efficient at covering their recklessness, and so on. Alternatively, it might also mean that the definition of DWI has changed or that the way arrests are recorded has changed. Measuring each of these facets of the law enforcement system related to drinking and driving would elucidate the reasons for the increase (Figure 2.1).

More reasonably, and feasibly, local community system effects may be averaged over geographic units (assuming, for example, that not every community will have an enforcement crackdown at the same time), arrests may be triangulated with other outcomes (e.g., arrests for public drunkenness), or measures may be sought that are believed to remain uncontaminated by system effects (e.g., single vehicle nighttime crashes). Following this logic, analyses of the influence of differential alcohol availability at the state and community levels have "averaged across" much local variation, showing that the physical availability of alcohol is related to levels of use (Gruenewald, Ponicki, & Holder, 1993) and arrests for alcohol-related problems (DWI and public drunkenness; Watts & Rabow, 1983). Similarly, studies of the effect of police crackdowns on drunk driving rates—a situation in which arrest measures must increase—have used a surrogate for DWI not directly influenced by local variations in enforcement rates (e.g., single-vehicle nighttime crashes; Ross, 1982).

SYSTEMS MODELS AND PUBLIC HEALTH

So much public discussion of drug and alcohol problems is dominated by facile metaphor and slogan—e.g., the "war" on drugs, the crack "epidemic," "demand" versus "supply" reduction—that it is sometimes difficult to grasp the complexities of community systems that support these problems. Superficial metaphors lead to superficial solutions:

> Winning the war on drugs calls for the reinforcement of those at the front (e.g., local, state, national, and international interdiction efforts).

> Stopping the crack epidemic calls for treatment of crack abusers and prevention of the spread of this "disease" (e.g., through education efforts).

The bitter fruits of programs built on slogans, of course, are their disheartening failures in the community. Drug interdiction efforts have, on the whole, made little difference in the price and availability of cocaine in the United States (Johnson et al., 1990; Reuter, 1992), crack abusers still regularly cycle on and off the treatment roles (Department of Health and Human Services, 1992), and the effects of educational programs to reduce the demand for alcohol and drugs, particularly among young people, have been marginal at best (Moskowitz, 1989).

Like the rest of society, many in the scientific community would like to offer simple solutions to alcohol and drug problems. And, like the rest of society, scientists are subject to the compelling force of metaphor. Metaphor in scientific discourse is considerably more abstract than metaphor in everyday conversation, but nevertheless, it can be equally misleading. Metaphors from epidemiological and public health perspectives have come to dominate discourse in research into drug and alcohol problems. Thus, much scientific discussion of alcohol and drug problems is centered on elucidations of the etiology of alcohol and drug "disorders," rather than the social ontogeny of alcohol and drug problems. Unfortunately, the use of metaphor in the description of social problems has particular risks in that it encourages modes of thinking about social problems based on inappropriate uses of the medical and public health models.

The Medical and Public Health Models

It is helpful to put the current state of our knowledge of community indicators into context by considering two alternative models to the systems perspective argued here. The *medical model* views problems as rooted in the genetic and physiological composition of individuals. Public health problems, and consequently their solutions, are seen as the products and properties of individuals. The problem with the medical model as applied to social problems is several-fold. First, it views problems as "owned" by individuals. To the extent that the focus is on "the ill," the social etiology of illness is not recognized. Second, the solutions to problems are ultimately seen as involving changing the individual. Here the palliative is individual, not social, reform.

An illustration of the medical model as applied to social problems may be found in the history of the disease concept of alcoholism. Although the disease concept of alcoholism dates from the founding of the American republic, its fullest development may be found in the Alcoholics Anonymous (AA) movement, which emerged after the repeal of Prohibition, and the subsequent "medicalization" of alcohol-related problems. According to the view held by this movement and institutionalized within the medical and treatment professions, the problem is not, as argued by prohibitionists, in the drink. Rather, it is in the drinker. The power of the medical imagery may be found in the World Health Organization's 1957 Expert Committee on Addiction-Producing Drugs characterization of addiction in terms of (1) an overpowering desire or need (compulsion) to continue taking the drug and to obtain it by any means; (2) a tendency to increase the dose; (3) a psychic (psychological) and generally a physical dependence on the effects of the drug; (4) a detrimental effect on the individual and society (Levine, 1978). A similar pattern of thought may be found in successive attempts to provide various schemata for drug-related medical disorders (e.g., ICD-9-CM diagnostic categories).

The *public health model* was developed as an alternative to the medical model. This model shifts the emphasis from the individual to the environment in which the individual operates. Moreover, the public health model shifts the focus from individual manifestations (e.g., the tubercular individual) to social manifestations of a disease (e.g., rates of tuberculosis). According to a simplified version of this model, diseases are agents carried by individuals or hosts. Hosts then spread these agents to other hosts through an environmentally based process. This model may be illustrated by considering the spread of chicken pox among grade school students. According to the model, an agent (the viral infection) is carried by some host (individuals infected with the virus) who spreads the disease to other individuals by some environmentally based process (e.g., interpersonal contacts). In this version of the model, the agent and host are discrete organisms sharing a common environment. It is the interaction of agents and hosts within the environment that determines "vectors" of disease transmission (e.g., routine activities that bring together groups of uninfected and infected young people).

Clearly, the major contribution of the public health model has been its application to the spread of infectious diseases. This model shifts attention away from ill individuals to the environmental conditions that lead to the spread of illness. Unfortunately, the more general public health version of this model, the one often applied to alcohol or drug problems, takes the same conceptual approach, redefining the notions of disease and environment to include far broader aspects of human behavior. Thus, the concept of disease is expanded to include public health "problems" and the concept of the environment is expanded to include not only vectors of disease transmission but the culture as a whole. In this way, "public health problems" come to include a broad panoply of social problems that appear in the United States (e.g., crime, domestic violence, school failure). Whole cultures become environments in which individuals are at risk by virtue of their membership (e.g., subcultures of violence, Parker, 1993).

The intended outcome of this conceptualization of social problems is a broad expansion of the intellectual domain of the health sciences (see the "medicalization" of deviance, Rosenberg & Golden, 1992). The unintended outcome of this way of thinking is the misconceptualization of the problems themselves. Public health problems have come to include an enormous variety of behaviors with dubious roots in the genetic or physiological composition of individuals. These range from public health behaviors of broad public interest (e.g., smoking, alcohol, and illegal drug use), in which addictive processes appear to underlie continued use, to problems of equally broad public interest, in which physiological bases or addictive processes may or may not be involved (e.g., acts of interpersonal violence).[1] Moreover, this continuous redefinition of problems to fit the public health perspective has resulted in some rather peculiar bureaucratic juxtapositions: Thus, the Centers for Disease Control and Prevention (CDC) has come to sponsor a violence initiative under the presumption that violence is a preventable "disease" (National Center for Injury Prevention and Control, 1993). This process of continual redefinition has also resulted in the undermining of the original agent-host-environment model itself.

As it is applied to issues ever further afield of its original intent, the agent-host-environment model moves from a broad conceptual model of disease transmission to an extended metaphor. Thus, moving only a little bit afield of the model's original focus by contrasting its application to juvenile versus adult onset diabetes, the terms of the model can be seen to stretch and break. Juvenile onset diabetes is a genetically based fatal disorder inherited from one's biological parents. Genetically related individuals are the hosts of the disease, the genes themselves can be considered the agents (see Williams, 1992, p. 15), and the environments in which the disease is communicated are those biological systems by which genes are passed on from generation to generation. Adult onset diabetes, on the other hand, is a more complex disease in which genetic predispositions interact with environmental conditions to produce impairment (much like heart disease and cancer). The genetic components of this disorder are necessary for its appearance. The nutritive environment of the individual determines its manifestation. Thus, the incidence of adult onset diabetes is up to five times the U.S. average among Mexican Americans in the Southwest, as these new residents take on new diets unusually heavy in fats, sugars, and other carbohydrates (Diamond, 1992). Not genetically predisposed to metabolize large quantities of carbohydrates, these adults are at risk of becoming diabetic as they come to adapt to the lifestyles of a society in which these foods are readily and widely available.

The questions to be posed at this point regard the distinctions between agents, hosts, and environments: Is the agent the genetic constitution of individuals at risk, or is it the social and environmental circumstances in which these individuals find themselves? Are the hosts of the disease individuals genetically prone to adult onset diabetes or the environment that houses the food stuffs that support disease onset? In the case of adult onset diabetes, the conceptual separation of agents, hosts, and environments breaks down.

Extending the model to the most popular drug in the United States, alcohol, one could construe the agent for the disease of alcoholism to be the genotype underlying propensities to chronic drinking (the genetic component).[2] The environment provides the nutritive conditions (e.g., access to alcohol) in which this disease may appear. As in the case of adult onset diabetes, however, it is very difficult to separate out agents and hosts in the disease process. It is difficult to ascertain the degree to which any individual "has" the disease of alcoholism because incidence of the disease itself is so conditional on environmental circumstance. Insofar as the links between genetic predispositions and environmental conditions are the behaviors of individuals (e.g., choosing to drink), the model does not clearly apply.

Nevertheless, it is feasible to continue to defend the basic public health model by continuing to stretch the metaphor: The hosts of the disease of alcoholism may be individuals carrying the relevant genetic predispositions, and the environment may be anything that affects transmission of this genetic information through the gene pool. Alternatively, taking a coevolutionary approach, the agent may be cultural concepts supporting the use of alcohol ("memes," Dawkins, 1982). In this case, hosts might include individuals carrying and transmitting these concepts, and the environment would be aspects of the social, psychological, economic, and physical world that affect interactions among or provide means of transmitting information between individuals.

Finally, the model could be generalized to a population base (Holder & Wallack, 1986) in which the agent is alcohol use itself (social behaviors), the host is the human population in which these behaviors take place, and the environment is the social, economic, physical, and psychological circumstances of drinking environments (e.g., other drinkers and drinking contexts).[3] At this point, of course, the metaphor has become meaningless. The agent may be genes, ideas, alcohol, or people. The host may be an individual or a population, and the environment will be whatever else is left, including the behaviors of other hosts. In sum, the public health model has made two major historical contributions. First, it has sensitized us to the social or environmental factors underlying public health problems. Second, and as a result, it has shifted our attention from the examination of individual manifestations of public health problems to the social or collective manifestations. Ultimately, however, it has failed to provide clear criteria for classification of factors as agents, hosts, and environments. Perhaps the popularity of the model has been due to its tautologic applicability. Virtually any social phenomenon or condition can be considered an agent, a host, or a part of the environment, depending on the intellectual or political predilections of the person using it. Unfortunately, the model leaves practitioners with three empty conceptual boxes into which various social phenomena may be grouped.

The Systems Perspective

In fairness to the public health model, its failings stem not from any inability to account for the transmission of disease but rather from its application to social phenomena that have been misconceptualized as diseases. Accounting for the transmission of small pox, where it is possible to speak precisely of vectors and clearly defined pathologies, is both intellectually and scientifically a fundamentally different sort of enterprise than accounting for patterns of alcohol or drug use and related problems.

Is it possible to develop public health models that do not rely on the agent-host-environment model? As argued by Holder and Wallack (1986), a *systems perspective* on alcohol (and drug) use can go a long way in reducing some of the conceptual confusion that arises in applying standard public health models to the understanding of alcohol and drug problems. To a great extent, the systems perspective is useful because it takes a neutral stance with respect to valuations of the problems themselves. Alcoholism and other drug addiction may or may not be diseases, but they are generally accepted as public health problems. That is, individuals who are labeled as *alcoholic* or *drug addicted* create direct and indirect costs for society not presented by other individuals.

An explanation of how human behaviors come to be labeled *public health problems* is not the province of the systems perspective. Rather, a systems perspective examines aspects of individual behavioral and social systems to ascertain their functional roles in supporting and/or preventing problems themselves. In this sense, the systems approach has much in common with behavioral ecology—the exploration of the individual, social, and environmental dynamics that underlie human behavior (Smith & Winterhalder, 1992). As is the case for alcoholism and other drug addiction, some of these behaviors may or may not be clearly genetically based, but they are all assumed to arise through a dynamic interaction of individual, social, and environmental factors.

In terms of community-based studies of alcohol and drug problems, the systems perspective encourages researchers to examine individual and social behaviors that characterize consumption of these substances and, most important, locate these behaviors within community contexts. These community contexts reflect components of general community systems, the same community systems that produce community indicators.

Thus, a systems approach to the study of cocaine abuse might begin with an exploration of the social dynamics underlying initiation to use (e.g., peer group and family influences), expand to cover the social dynamics of obtaining cocaine (including economic models of the market for illegal drugs), continue with explorations of treatment-seeking behavior and the availability of treatment services, and conclude with an exploration of the punitive dynamics of policing and criminal sanctions for illegal purchases and use. The study would touch on many major community systems, including the educational system (where young people may come in contact with distributors of illegal drugs), the local illegal economy (where illegal drugs are marketed, distributed, and sold), the treatment service system, and the criminal justice system.

Cocaine abuse would be understood in terms of the major individual, social, and economic forces underlying its genesis and maintenance, a valuable summative goal in and of itself. But more important, the approach would begin to explicate how community systems come to bear directly on the problem. For example, how the criminal justice system acts to alter the illegal economy for drugs would become an essential part of the information about how individuals obtain cocaine to maintain abuse (e.g., availability).

In escaping the bounds of the agent-host-environment model, the systems perspective offers two advantages to the field of community studies of drug and alcohol problems. First, the valuative definition of problems themselves is no longer dependent on a disease metaphor. Problems are what communities define them to be. Second, the weak notion of the environment presented from a naive public health perspective is replaced with a stronger notion of the environment in terms of the functional operations of community systems and behavioral-functional aspects of the problems themselves. Thus, considering alcoholism again, the collection of alcohol-related problems clinicians come to label as symptomatic of alcoholism can be viewed as appearing in particular environmental contexts that promote the frequent heavy use of alcohol (e.g., those environments that protect users from mortality due to acute use), arising from the behavioral and social functions necessary to procure and consume alcohol (e.g., shopping for alcohol, choosing a place to drink, learning to drink safely at work), and aggravated by the association of alcohol with other life activities (e.g., commuting to work).

From a systems perspective, alcohol and drug problems arise in environmental contexts and are inseparable from them. It is in frank recognition of the contingent nature of social behavior that the systems perspective gains its power and flexibility. A problem is not a problem only when society defines it to be so, but also a problem insofar as the behavioral, social, and environmental contingencies support its manifestation.

SUMMARY

This chapter began with a discussion of the social indicators movement, which served as an early precursor to the current community indicators movement. In general, the chapter concludes that the failure of this movement was due to the absence of both a theoretical basis and associated data collection and analysis techniques. It proceeded to discuss three alternative models of social problems: the medical model, the public health model, and the systems perspective model. The systems model appears to be the most likely to produce a coherent theoretical framework for community indicators collection and analysis. In the next chapter, we discuss the practical implications of systems modeling for such work and present as an extended illustration a community-level computer simulation.

NOTES

1. As generally defined, *addictions* in this context are considered to be patterns of use that are difficult for the individual to alter or reduce and that may lead to physiological symptoms of withdrawal on discontinued use. The term has been used in rational economic theory to describe temporal autocorrelations of use implying the presence of habit (Grossman, 1991). In this naive and somewhat absurd sense, a conditionally dependent preference for mussels in red pepper sauce is addictive. It is also worthy of note here that physiological symptoms of withdrawal appear on the discontinued regular use of caffeine, nicotine, alcohol, and a host of other drugs.

2. The term *disease* is used advisedly in this context. There is considerable uncertainty among researchers as to whether the behavioral symptoms that accompany the chronic abuse of alcohol should be ascribed this conceptual status (*British Journal of Addiction,* 1987).

3. Early arguments for a systems perspective on alcohol problems supported a population-based approach in contradistinction to a disease (individual) approach. This distinction is not a necessary one, but is valuable for the purpose of clarifying the differences in these two public health approaches to these issues (Holder & Wallack, 1986).

3

Systems Models and Society

What precedent is there for the development of systems models in the social sciences? Is there reason to believe that such models can be properly applied to alcohol and other drug issues? This chapter explores these issues by reviewing the current state of systems theory. It concludes with an extensive discussion of SIMCOM, an application of systems modeling principles and techniques to alcohol and drug use and problems.

SYSTEMS MODELS IN THE BEHAVIORAL SCIENCES

For the past 20 years, the application of large-scale systems models in the social sciences has been predominantly the domain of macroeconomics (Klein, 1991; MacRae, 1985). Although sociologists and criminologists have begun to develop macrosociological models of social and criminal behavior (e.g., Maltz, 1984; Tuma & Hannan, 1984), these models are currently restricted to focal areas (e.g., political structure, social diffusion processes, recidivism) in which the global complexities of social processes can be ignored. Furthermore, these models have often been constructed using readily available data independent of theoretical considerations. As shown by the progress made by macroeconomic models of the U.S. economy (Klein, 1991), a theoretically driven or synthetic approach to model development can be beneficial to both an understanding of the complex dynamics of economic systems and the limits of underlying theories of economic behavior (see also MacRae, 1985). Such an approach, however, requires a careful theoretic development of the processes assumed to underlie the outcome(s) of interest (e.g., performance of the U.S. economy), the indexing of these processes with available data from empirical analyses of the systems studied (e.g., retail activity, gross domestic product), and the simulation of the system to see whether or not the results of the model adequately mimic both qualitative and quantitative aspects of the systems studied.

In the case of alcohol and drug problems, a synthetic approach requires the development of systems models based on the best available theoretical and empirical models in the field. Taking this approach, the simulation of a variety of complex alcohol and drug problems has been touched on by a handful of authors over the past 20 years. These include system simulations of narcotics use by Levin, Roberts, and Hirsch (1975) and alcohol use and regulatory policy by Katzper, Ryback, and Hertzman (1976), and preliminary prototypes of more comprehensive alcohol use and problem models by Holder (1974), Hallan and Holder (1986a, 1986b), and Holder and Blose (1983, 1987). After a brief review of the work of these latter authors and the presentation of a demonstration of an application of this approach to drunk driving, the value of taking this approach to understanding community drug and alcohol problems can be better appreciated.

ISSUES IN SYSTEMS MODELING

By far, the most ambitious attempt to explicate community systems and their relationships to drug and alcohol problems is found in the work of Holder, Miner, and Kible (1993a, 1993b, 1993c).[1] Their development of SIMCOM (a SIMulated COMmunity model of alcohol use and abuse) represents a successful integration of both theory and empirical analysis for the simulation study of community-based alcohol problems. The goals of the modeling strategy are (1) to represent adequately the theoretical structure of community systems that come to bear on alcohol problems; (2) to incorporate into these theoretical-structural representations estimates of effects obtained from empirical research; and (3) to mimic the dynamics of community systems underlying alcohol problems. The procedure used in the application of the model is as follows. First, based on theoretically significant observations of social-structure relationships between community systems (e.g., the price charged by retailers for alcohol and the demand for this commodity), estimates of associations between community variables and outcomes are determined. To take a simple example, a review of the literature examining the relationship between alcohol price and consumption may indicate that for every 1% increase in the price of alcohol there will be a corresponding 1% decrease in alcohol consumption. This stage in the process is critical because it illustrates the a priori theoretical basis of the model and its overall synthetic character. In other words, it is driven by an underlying theoretical structure. This provides a sharp contrast to the data-driven attempts to model community systems discussed above. Second, time series for background variables of interest must be found for the community of interest—in the case presented here, alcohol price estimates and historic consumption levels. Third, expected values for alcohol consumption can be generated based on knowledge of alcohol prices by loading effect estimates into the model. So, for example, given a 2% decrease in price during a given year, we would predict a 2% increase in consumption over that time frame. Given information about consumption at any given point in time and information about subsequent price changes, times series estimates of subsequent alcohol consumption can be generated. These expected values can be compared to observed values and the model can be revised. Of course, actual computer models are much more complex and incorporate hundreds of variables in feedback loops characterized by complex mathematical relationships.

There are both soft and hard criteria of success for each of these endeavors, each considered in successive iterations of development of the model (see Holder et al., 1993a). From a soft perspective, the mere specification of a comprehensive formal model of the relationships among community systems bearing on alcohol problems is a substantial contribution to the field. The rigors of comprehensive systems modeling inevitably force investigators to address the weaknesses of theory in the face of facts. Gaps appear between subsystems, theory stretches only so far, and inadequacies in current thinking about the system at hand (e.g., relationships between various systems components) become painfully evident.

For similar reasons, and again from a soft perspective, qualitative relationships between community systems bearing on the problem, although obvious in principle, by no means may be obvious in fact. Thus, a successful model will enable qualitative explorations of community system interactions, and a soft criterion of its success would mimic the qualitative expectations of system interactions based on a priori theoretical considerations. To the extent that such models achieve these minimal soft goals, their face validity remains intact (for an interesting exploration of macroeconomic models from this point of view, see Adams & Klein, 1991).

From a hard perspective, simulation models must meet the rigors implied by the second and third goals of the approach—the successful introduction of empirical estimates of effects into the models and mimicking the dynamics of actual community systems. These goals are difficult to achieve for a number of reasons. First, the introduction of empirical estimates of effects from the literature into comprehensive, theoretically based models of community systems requires that these estimates be made under equivalent structural conditions. In other words, the estimates introduced into a model for one community should be, to the extent possible, generated from a community similar in relevant characteristics. This can be illustrated by considering the implementation of our simple simulation model examining the relationship between alcohol price and alcohol consumption. Assuming for the moment a community in which purchasing cheaper brands in the face of increasing prices is common, one would find that the effect of price on consumption levels would be relatively low. The application or loading of this small effect parameter in a model for a community where such purchase substitutions are rare would not be appropriate.

An additional problem concerns the fact that the development of social and economic models with the greatest degree of fidelity to theoretical frames and empirical fact generates models of great complexity. The unavailability of adequate data to test these models comprehensively renders the power of these tests less than would be desirable otherwise. Thus, one often sees models of enormous complexity tested against outcomes measured over periods of only a few decades (Holder & Blose, 1987; Klein, 1991). One way of addressing the problem of too many variables and too few cases is to test subcomponents of the models as thoroughly as possible before integrating them into the framework of the entire simulation. In this way, tests of the performance of subcomponents of the model support tests of the model as a whole.

Holder et al. (1993a, 1993b, 1993c) have taken this approach. Holder and his colleagues consider each subcomponent of their model of community alcohol use and abuse as subsystems of interactions between individuals and functional community systems. These systems constitute important components of the environment of individuals. Although often crudely represented in the model, they begin to address issues of the emergence of alcohol problems in the context of social systems in which individuals play essential, but not exclusive, roles.

Figure 3.1 presents an overview of the causal model introduced by Holder et al. (1993a, 1993b, 1993c). The overall model consists of eight interacting subsystems. These include (1) a consumption subsystem that represents the distribution of consumption patterns in the community population, (2) a retail market subsystem that represents the marketing and distribution of alcohol through the community, (3) a formal regulations and control subsystem that represents formal regulatory interventions

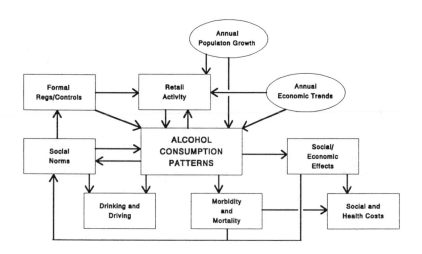

Figure 3.1. Causal Model of Alcohol Use and Alcohol-Related Trauma

expected to affect alcohol distribution and consumption patterns (e.g., minimum drinking age, planning, and zoning laws), (4) a social norms subsystem that represents, among other things, ethnic and sociocultural determinants of drinking patterns, (5) a drinking and driving subsystem that represents the distribution of driving events at different blood alcohol levels in the community and may be mapped into numbers of driver fatalities and injury crashes, (6) a mortality and morbidity subsystem that represents other sources of alcohol-related mortality and morbidity (e.g., drownings and falls), (7) a social and economic consequences subsystem that represents the effect of alcohol use on family and workplace networks, and (8) a social and health services subsystem that represents the effect of alcohol use on community social and health services.

As seen in Figure 3.1, these subsystems themselves are complexly interrelated. For example, the figure portrays sets of recursive (unidirectional) and nonrecursive (bidirectional) relationships between the social norms, formal regulations and controls, retail activity, and alcohol consumption patterns subsystems. Social norms are conceived as directly affecting formal regulations and controls, and these regulations are conceived as directly affecting retail activity and alcohol consumption patterns, representing a block recursive system. On the other hand, alcohol consumption patterns may affect retail activity in the alcohol market, placing pressure on retailers to open more alcohol outlets, and retail activity in the market may increase physical availability of alcohol affecting alcohol consumption patterns, representing two block non-recursive subsystems. (For an elementary discussion of block recursive systems, see Wonnacott & Wonnacott, 1979. For more complete discussions of modeling and estimation issues in mixed block recursive and nonrecursive systems, see Greene, 1993, and Judge, Griffiths, Hill, Lutkepohl, & Lee, 1985.) Thus, either subsystems may directly affect other subsystems and not be acted on by these subsystems in turn (i.e., recursive systems) or subsystems may nonrecursively affect each other.

As a practical example, consider the case of raising and lowering the minimum drinking age. One could argue that the social norms of a community would at least in part determine the likelihood of raising, or lowering, the minimum drinking age. For example, in the desire to reduce alcohol consumption, particularly among young people, more conservative states might raise the minimum drinking age, whereas less conservative states might be disinclined to do so. Thus, social norms would directly affect changes in formal regulation, represented by the arrow directed from the former to the latter subsystem. Furthermore, one could argue that an increase in the minimum drinking age law would directly affect both retail activity (lowering sales to young people) and alcohol consumption patterns (lowering use among young people), represented by the arrows directed from the formal regulation subsystem to the retail activity and consumption patterns subsystems. Thus, social norms and formal regulations could be conceived to have direct, recursive, effects on retail activity and alcohol use. In addition, decreases in retail activity resulting from increases in the minimum drinking age law (e.g., the closing of alcohol outlets) could be conceived as decreasing alcohol consumption through decreased access to alcohol, whereas decreases in the demand for alcohol—through direct effects of changes in formal regulation on alcohol demand—could be conceived as placing downward pressure on retail activity in the alcohol market (e.g., through decreased sales and increased competition between current outlets). Thus, these two subsystems of the model may be conceived to affect each other nonrecursively, as shown by the reciprocally pointing sets of arrows between them. Finally, completing the cycle portrayed in Figure 3.1, decreases in alcohol consumption among young people may result in direct alterations in social norms as concern for drinking among young people eases in the community.[2]

As shown in Figure 3.1, the four components of SIMCOM discussed above each bear directly (the social norms and alcohol consumption subsystems) or indirectly (the formal regulations and retail activities subsystems) on drinking and driving. The drinking and driving subsystem itself is conceived as affecting probabilities of morbidity and mortality and, subsequently, social norms, completing another conceptual cycle in the model. Moreover, one needs to remember that each of these system components is itself a subsystem with its own components.

THE USES OF SYSTEMS THEORETIC MODELS

Much of the success of complex systems models rests on their ability to capture both theoretical structure and the results of empirical research in their implementation. In the absence of either, the modelers are sometimes called on to improvise. Thus, the strongest challenge to model building in complex systems such as community systems related to drug and alcohol abuse is to represent the theoretical views and empirical observations of researchers in the varying contexts of real-world events (MacRae, 1985). At the very least, attempts to build comprehensive models of community systems lead to a recognition of the limits of our current knowledge of how communities work.

It is in the nature of complex systems that causal inputs and outputs are often mutually reinforcing or nonrecursive. Thus, decreases in the price of alcohol may lead to increases in consumption that, by decreasing the per unit production cost, lead to further price decreases. As shown by the discussion of the SIMCOM model above, recursive, nonrecursive, and cyclic nonrecursive patterns of relationships among subsystems and their components can be observed. It is likely that these kinds of relationships characterize much of the interactive structure of community systems.

As systems grow more complex, their fidelity to the realities of community events improves while the separability of exogenous and endogenous factors becomes more problematic. This increase in complexity is accompanied by a decrease in the applicability of standard experimental procedures to the evaluation of community systems themselves, leading researchers to analytic paradigms that reflect the complexities of the problems at hand (Klitzner, 1994). Thus, it is no surprise to see the increasing application of multiequation (one equation for each endogenous measure or effect) models to the evaluation of preventive interventions in ever more realistic contexts (Gruenewald, Ponicki, & Holder, 1993; Saffer & Grossman, 1987).

As an example of the way in which theoretical structure and empirical data come to inform systems models, consider the relationships portrayed in Figure 3.1 between social norms, formal regulations and controls, retail activity, and alcohol consumption patterns. In this portion of the model, explicit recognition of (1) the theoretically expected and empirically observed relationships between social norms and regulatory processes (e.g., with regard to the minimum drinking age, Saffer & Grossman, 1987), (2) the theoretically expected and empirically observed relationship between regulatory forms and retail activity in the alcohol market (e.g., the influence of monopolization on availability, Gruenewald, Madden, & Janes, 1992), and (3) the simultaneous relationship between retail activity and alcohol sales (Gruenewald, Ponicki, & Holder, 1993) strengthens the descriptive adequacy of the model. Each of the three studies cited supports theoretical expectations for relationships between these subsystems of SIMCOM. Saffer and Grossman (1987) show that one surrogate for social norms (religious preferences) affects the likelihood of a change in the minimum drinking age over time. Gruenewald et al. (1992) demonstrate that state alcohol monopolies successfully limit the availability of spirits through the restrictive distribution of this beverage type, but that the availability of beer and wine expands in this context. Gruenewald, Ponicki, and Holder (1993) show that increased physical availability of alcohol (measured in terms of both population and geographic densities) is related to increases in alcohol sales, and, independently, that increased alcohol sales are related to increased availability (through the opening of new outlets to meet increased demand).

As an example of how the development of a comprehensive systems model points out the limitations of theoretical and empirical work, consider the relationship between alcohol consumption patterns and one formal regulatory mechanism—alcohol beverage taxes. Although most economists are in agreement that increased alcohol beverage taxes are likely to lead to some reduction in the use of alcohol (Chaloupka, 1993; Leung & Phelps, 1991), the relationship between tax increases and specific forms of consumption is only poorly understood. Some research has suggested that increased taxation may differentially affect heavy consumption (particularly of beer among young people, Coate & Grossman, 1988; Grossman, Coate, & Arluck, 1987), but no research has yet appeared specifically addressing the possible differential effect of taxes among the population of drinkers at large. Although it would be desirable that tax increases most affect the heaviest consumers of alcohol (presumably then having the greatest effect on drinking problems, Cook

& Moore, 1991), evidence to this effect is lacking. Consequently, in the absence of sufficient information regarding these relationships, SIM-COM assumes that the effect of tax increases is distributed evenly across all consumers regardless of consumption class (Holder et al., 1993a, 1993b, 1993c).

Another area in which SIMCOM demonstrates the limitations of current theory and empirical data is in the description of consumption patterns in the alcohol consumption patterns subsystem. SIMCOM assumes that total consumption is the standard by which consumption patterns across demographic groups are to be measured when, in fact, much literature on consumption patterns points toward more sophisti-cated models of alcohol use (e.g., Clark & Hilton, 1991; Gruenewald & Nephew, 1994). Thus, relationships between demographic background characteristics and consumption patterns can be quite variegated.

At the most rudimentary level, drinking patterns can be characterized by different frequencies of consumption and quantities consumed per occasion. Using this characterization, older consumers have been observed to drink more frequently than young consumers and drink less per occasion, higher levels of income have been shown to be related to greater frequen-cies of use but not quantities consumed, and increased educational levels have been related to decreases in quantities consumed but not frequencies of use (Gruenewald & Nephew, 1994). Despite these obser-vations, however, there is no explicit theory of how expectations regard-ing alcohol-related problems are to be mapped onto pattern measures of this kind (cf. Gruenewald & Nephew, 1991). For this reason, SIMCOM cannot introduce this more sophisticated approach to modeling alcohol consumption patterns into the structure of the model.

SUMMARY

As these examples show, systems theoretic models such as SIMCOM can be very informative from a purely qualitative point of view. Prob-lems in the implementation of these complex models indicate areas in which theory and empirical data fall short of the goal of explaining community systems and their relationships to alcohol and drug prob-lems. Furthermore, considering the global goal of explaining the roles of community indicators in the context of complex community systems, these mathematical representations of community systems appear to be the only adequate formulations available. Nowhere else is the necessary complexity of community systems captured with sufficient fidelity to the problems at hand.

As pointed out by McFarland (1975) when discussing the conceptual foundations of the social indicators movement, community indicators, for obvious reasons, refer to issues of concern to community members (e.g., arrests for drug possession and sales). These indicators can be used to index outcomes (e.g., the effectiveness of a policing strategy), evaluate community-level structural changes (e.g., increases in costs of alcohol), or evaluate planned policy interventions (e.g., changes in legal penalties for possession). Without adequate mathematical representations of the relationships of indicators to the social and economic systems they represent, however, their use is, at best, limited to guesses about the probable causes of change in the systems of interest.

In the absence of well-specified models of community systems, the meaning of substantive changes in community indicators remains vague and imprecise. To the degree that community indicators achieve clear and precise meanings in social and political systems, their contribution to our understanding of these systems will increase (Innes, 1990). It is our assertion here that the roles community indicators play in community systems can best be understood using adequate formal mathematical models of these relationships.

NOTES

1. We would like to express our appreciation to Drs. Holder and Kible for providing copies of the extensive, and currently unpublished, documentation of this simulation model.

2. The completion of the systems loop from the social norms subsystem through the formal regulation, retail activity, and consumption pattern subsystems and back again represents a block nonrecursive loop. An entertaining introductory discussion of such cyclical nonrecursive loops can be found in Kenny (1979).

4

Substance Use-Abuse Indicators

This chapter discusses a number of community indicators of alcohol and other drug use patterns and problems. Our specific focus is on the areas of crime, health, education, the economy, demographics, and politics— all of which have either affected or been affected by alcohol and drug use. In presenting this chapter, our intention is to provide both the rationale for using these indicators and necessary warnings about their use. Again, the fact that these indicators are produced by the communities themselves makes their careful scrutiny necessary.

THE SOCIAL INDICATORS
MOVEMENT REVISITED

In the heyday of the social indicators movement, a number of authors and publications were concerned with the accumulation and dissemination of information on available archival sources of social data. These span every level of geographic aggregation from the international (as represented by data available from the United Nations, 1989) down to the urban (Champagne, Crowe, Flaming, & Judd, 1976; Flax, 1978; Hughes, 1973) and suburban (e.g., based on census tract data, Adams, 1976), and reflect levels of temporal resolution from the decennial to the annual. Much of the available data had a number of limitations, perhaps the most serious of which were the limits of social measurement and specifications of the social meanings of the indicators themselves (Innes, 1990; MacRae, 1985). Compendia of indicators, although useful from an archival point of view, were not supported by well-specified models of the roles the indicators played in any system or systems. Viewing the contents of these early collections, one receives the same uncomfortable impression one would receive from viewing, and trying to make sense of, a randomly ordered set of elements from the periodic table. Whatever order may be imagined to underlie the elements, it is not evident in their presentation.

The past 20 years have seen considerable efforts to explore and explain alcohol and drug problems in a wide variety of settings. Results of these studies, although not without controversy, have provided the outlines of frameworks within which these problems can be understood. These conceptual frameworks provide, among other things, some structural meaning to indicators of alcohol and drug problems, placing them in the context of various social and economic systems. SIMCOM is a notable result of such work. As should also be evident from the approach taken here, however, a community systems perspective on alcohol and drug problems makes additional demands of indicators data. Useful indicators not only must be explicable within the context of community systems themselves, but must be appropriate in terms of geographic scale and temporal resolution (e.g., monthly, yearly). As Chapter 6 will show, a major problem for indicator collection and analysis concerns the need to find common spatial and time frames. Clearly, using monthly arrest data aggregated at the police precinct level to explain drug use data collected yearly at the school district level would violate the formal requirement that data share a common temporal and spatial resolution. Moreover, this sort of problem is quite common in community indicators analysis.

This chapter outlines some prominent indicators of alcohol and drug use-abuse that have been used in previous research and address important components of community systems. The list of indicators presented here is available at a geographic level of aggregation adequate to approximate the community (e.g., indicators available at the county, city, zip code, or census tract levels) and notes the availability of similar data at higher levels of aggregation. Although the list is far from exhaustive, it is indicative of the primary measures of concern in the analysis of community systems relevant to alcohol and drug problems. Once we have examined the properties of some available indicators, their roles in community systems models of alcohol and drug problems can be further developed.

Tables 4.1, 4.2, 4.5, and 4.6 present the outlines of the community indicators discussed here. Included in these tables are descriptions of the general areas that the indicators cover (crime, health, schools, economy, demographics, and politics), each reflecting either specific community systems (criminal justice, health care, educational, economic, and political) or general population variables (demographics). Where feasible, specific indicators within areas are mentioned (e.g., retail alcohol prices in the area of economy), some indication of the

Table 4.1

Crime Indicators

Area	Indicator	Expected Geographic Specificity	Expected Periodicity	Example Source
Crime	Drug arrests (sales and possession)	Beat/police jurisdiction/city	Monthly/annually	Local police dept./ State crime information centers
	Drunk driving arrest	Beat/police jurisdiction/city	Monthly/annually	Local police dept./ state crime information centers
	Liquor law violations	Beat/police jurisdiction/city	Monthly/annually	Local police dept./ state crime information centers
	Drunkenness arrests	Beat/police jurisdiction/city	Monthly/annually	Local police dept./ state crime information centers
	Full-time law enforcement officers	Beat/police jurisdiction/city	Monthly/annually	Local police dept./ state crime information centers

geographic specificity and temporal resolution are noted, and a sample source or sources are presented. These examples will help readers guide their searches through community sources for indicators and facilitate later discussion of the roles such indicators can play in understanding community systems.

Crime

Table 4.1 presents an outline of some typical indicators of crime related to drug and alcohol use. These indicators are almost exclusively constituted of measures of arrest. Because arrests arise through the joint actions of criminals and enforcement officers, a supplemental measure of enforcement potential (full-time law enforcement officers) is included.

The use of arrest data as a presumed outcome of crime and enforcement rates has been a standard in criminological research for the better part of the 20th century (e.g., see Maltz, 1984; Sellin, 1931; Sellin & Wolfgang, 1964). Arrest data are generally preferred to measures of police calls and conviction rates. Calls to police represent the characterization of an apparently criminal act in terms of the caller's view of the problem. On brief investigation, what was called in as a car theft could well turn out to be a lost car. At the other extreme, actions of the criminal justice system filter measures of criminal events to the point where alternative measures of crime (e.g., convictions) may be more representative of legal maneuvering (e.g., pleading down) than the crimes themselves. Although measures of arrest represent no panacea, it is generally conceded that they represent the best compromise between these two sources of bias.

Arrest data of the kind presented here are widely available throughout the United States. Participation of local police departments in the FBI's Uniform Crime Reporting system supports the collection of index crime data, much of which specifically covers drug and alcohol-related arrests. Thus, measures of drug arrests (e.g., sales and possession), drunk driving arrests (varying, among other things, by the legal blood alcohol levels of different jurisdictions), liquor law violations (e.g., sales to minors), and arrests for public drunkenness can be obtained from reporting police jurisdictions throughout the country. The geographies of these jurisdictions are often concurrent with city boundaries, thus clearly representing communities at this level of aggregation, and data can sometimes be obtained at the level of jurisdiction "beats" (i.e., specific police subdivisions of the community). Data are almost invariably available on an annual basis, frequently on a quarterly basis, and less frequently on a monthly basis from each jurisdiction.

Costs of data collection for arrest data are, on the face of it, nominal. Within resource constraints, police jurisdictions are almost invariably willing to cooperate with researchers to provide these data. Increased costs to the researcher often accrue through variations in legal definitions from jurisdiction to jurisdiction (e.g., legal blood alcohol levels defining drunk driving, differences in the legal definition of drug categories, and possession and sale events) and associated attempts to resolve these definitional issues by (1) clarification of legal definitions, (2) aggregating the data up to a level in which a common definition appears to occur, such as "all drug arrests," or (3) otherwise coding definitional differences in the process of data acquisition (e.g., developing a parallel model of the formal law, see Gruenewald, Madden, & Janes, 1992; Janes & Gruenewald, 1991).

Further operational costs of acquiring and using arrest data are reflected in the last indicator noted under the area of crime in Table 4.1. There, the measurement of full-time law enforcement officers is included to provide a crude measure of enforcement pressure in measured arrest rates. As noted earlier, focused enforcement of drug control laws can increase drug-related arrest rates (Kleiman & Smith, 1990). Short of knowing the distribution of annual beat assignments by jurisdiction over each year of arrest data acquisition, there is no feasible strategy for determining differential enforcement pressures by jurisdiction. Often the best one can do is measure numbers of available field officers by jurisdiction.

Applications

Some notable examples of the use of arrest indicators in studies of alcohol-related problems appear in the work of Rush and Gliksman (1986), Rush, Gliksman, and Brook (1986), and Watts and Rabow (1983). Although these authors fail to account for possible arrest differentials arising through differences in law enforcement efforts, they do demonstrate how multiple arrest measures can be used to ascertain the effect of changes in alcohol policy (e.g., differences in alcohol availability). As a group, these studies suggest that reductions in the total availability of alcohol will reduce rates of arrest for both drunk driving and public drunkenness, whereas changes in forms of availability will differentially affect these rates. Thus, Watts and Rabow (1983) show that reductions in numbers of on-premise establishments such as bars and restaurants have a particularly strong effect on rates of arrest for public drunkenness, but no substantial effect on arrests for drunk driving.

Although national reports of arrest rates and self-reports of illegal drug use have been a staple of research for some time, current studies of drug-related arrests increasingly have tended to focus on smaller population aggregates. Because illegal drug use, as opposed to alcohol use, is illegal per se, the visibility of drug-related activities tends to be relatively low. Neither manufacturers, importers, wholesalers, retailers, nor users wish their activities publicized, and all actively seek invisibility to police action. Thus, studies of local community drug enforcement activities have come to the forefront of drug-related criminological research; these studies have come to rely on alternative sources of information on drug-related crime (e.g., ethnographic studies, reports of victimization rates, and personal criminal involvement, Chaiken & Chaiken, 1990). To the extent that arrest rates remain a topic of central relevance to these studies, they do so as measures of the intervention effectiveness of police action (Kleiman & Smith, 1990) and potential reduction in the availability or supply of drugs (Moore, 1990), not as measures of the outcome of such actions.

As noted by Kleiman and Smith (1990), the number of criminal events in which illegal drug users participate (including use itself) is astronomical. No doubt the ratio of illegal events to arrests is similarly large. In light of this observation, arrests for illegal drug sales and use may be more closely tied to enforcement action than actual criminal activity. In this case, use of arrest data as surrogates for crime rates should be greeted with some skepticism. When used in conjunction with other sources of information on crime rates (e.g., self-reports of victimization) and/or measures of enforcement pressure, however, rates of arrest for drug-related crimes can prove a valuable adjunct to models of the effect of police efforts (see Moore, 1990).

Health

Using the state of California as an illustration, Table 4.2 presents an outline of some typical indicators of health events related to drug and alcohol use.[1] These data consist of mortality and morbidity measures. The mortality measures come from either police reporting systems designed to track specific traffic-related events or death certificate data. Traffic fatality data are recorded by local police authorities, passed on to state administrators, and again passed on to the National Highway Traffic Safety Administration's (NHTSA) Fatal Accident Reporting System (FARS; NHTSA, 1992). Death certificate data are collected at the local level from city and county coroner's offices, passed on to state administrators, and passed on again to the National Center for Health Statistics and made available by them in the form of the Mortality Detail Files (National Center for Health Statistics, 1992).

Morbidity measures are generally more difficult to obtain and may be available exclusively at the state or local level. Traffic crash data are usually maintained at the state level and serve as the basis in most states for data sent on to the FARS (e.g., the state of California's Statewide Integrated Traffic Records System, 1993). Health-related morbidity measures are also frequently available at the state level in the form of hospital discharge data from private, state, and other public institutions (e.g., the California Hospital Discharge Data Program, 1993). Measures of infant mortality and tuberculosis incidence are included here as health indicators related to regional impoverishment.

Table 4.2

Health Indicators

Area	Indicator	Expected Geographic Specificity	Expected Periodicity	Example Source
Health	Single-vehicle fatal crashes	Street level/ city/ county/ state	Daily/monthly	National Highway Traffic Safety Administration Fatal Accident Reporting System (FARS)
	Single-vehicle crashes	City/county/ state	Daily/monthly	California Traffic Reporting System
	Mortality due to alcohol abuse	Street Level/ city/county/ zip/state	Daily/monthly	National Center for Health Statistics (NCHS) mortality tapes
	Mortality due to drug abuse	City/county/ zip/state	Daily/monthly	NCHS mortality tapes
	Tuberculosis incidence	Street level/ zip	Daily/monthly/ biannually	Office of Statewide Hospital and Planning Department
	Alcohol and drug treatment services	County/zip	Monthly/ annually	California alcohol and drug data

As noted earlier, traffic crashes are a frequent outcome of the use of alcohol in combination with driving. Current estimates are that 47% of all fatal traffic crashes involved alcohol to some degree (Evans, 1990; 18.2 per 100,000, Aitken & Zobeck, 1985). For this reason, fatal traffic crash rates are often used as a surrogate for drunk driving in state-level analyses of the effect of various preventive interventions on alcohol-related mortality rates (e.g., Saffer & Grossman, 1987). The primary benefit arising from the use of this surrogate is its detachment from contaminating fluctuations in enforcement rates often observed in arrest data (Ross, 1982). To the extent that such fatality measures can be further focused on single-vehicle nighttime driving, their specificity to drunk driving increases (Gruenewald & Ponicki, 1995b).

Although alcohol involvement in fatal vehicle crashes is relatively high, the use of fatal crashes as a surrogate for alcohol-related vehicle crash mortality is problematic. Because fatal crashes are relatively rare at county and community levels, this measure provides neither sufficient or stable numbers of observations over time. Thus, the preferred measure by most traffic researchers is single-vehicle nighttime crashes (i.e., those with only one moving vehicle and occurring between 8 pm and 4 am), filtered to remove commercial vehicles, motorcycles, animal- and pedestrian-involved crashes, and bicycle crashes. Estimates of alcohol involvement in single-vehicle nighttime crashes rise to as high as 80% during the later driving hours (Zador et al., 1988). This measure provides more observations per unit than fatal crashes and has been shown to include a significant number of alcohol-involved drivers (Mounce, Pendleton, & Gonzales, 1988; Richman, 1985). It is sensitive to changes in alcohol use and availability in studies of the minimum purchase age (Wagenaar, 1986a, 1986b), changes in spirits availability (Blose & Holder, 1987), and changes in beverage server liability (Wagenaar & Holder, 1991).

Although mortality data available from death certificates may include some biases in reporting (e.g., coroner's preferences to underreport certain causes of death, i.e., alcoholism), death certificate data include an indication of the primary cause of death that may be used to establish mortality related to drug and alcohol use. Multiple causes of death, although sometimes available, appear to be relatively poorly coded. Of course, this consideration must be weighed against the loss of information associated with using only the primary cause of death.

The current standard coding scheme used in reporting mortality data comes from the international classification of diseases used by the World Health Organization (Puckett, 1992) and, as shown in Tables 4.3 and 4.4, deaths related to alcohol and drugs can be specifically defined. The most often reported causes of death related to alcohol use are cirrhosis and other liver damage (571.0, 571.2, 571.3, 571.5). These causes of death occur at an approximate national rate of 4.4 per 100,000 individuals per year (or 1/4 of the rate for alcohol-related fatal crashes, Williams et al., 1988). Focusing on drug-related deaths, the most frequent causes are those due to poisoning (E850.0 through E854.2). These causes of death occur at an approximate national rate of .35 per 100,000 individuals per year (or 1/52 of the rate for alcohol related fatal crashes, Baker et al., 1992).

The very low base rates of mortality related to drug and alcohol use and abuse suggests that these measures may have only very limited utility in community-based studies of alcohol and drug problems. Although researchers have investigated relationships between cirrhosis mortality rates and alcohol beverage sales and availability at the state level (e.g.,

Table 4.3

Mortality Due to Alcohol Abuse (ICD-9-CM)

Code		Definition
303		Alcohol dependence syndrome
	303.0	Acute alcohol intoxication
	303.9	Other and unspecified alcohol dependence
305.0		Alcohol abuse (nondependent)
425.5		Alcoholic cardiomyopathy
456.0		Esophageal varices with bleeding
	456.1	Esophageal varices without bleeding
	456.2	Esophageal varices in diseases classified elsewhere
535.3		Alcohol gastritis
571		Chronic liver disease and cirrhosis
	571.0	Alcohol fatty liver
	571.1	Acute alcohol hepatitis
	571.2	Alcoholic cirrhosis of liver
	571.3	Alcoholic liver damage unspecified
	571.5	Cirrhosis of liver without mention of alcohol
572		Liver abscess and sequelae of chronic liver disease
980.0		Toxic effect of alcohol (ethyl, e.g., grain alcohol)
V11.3		Alcoholism
E860.0		Accidental poisoning by alcohol for consumption
E860.1		Accidental poisoning by alcohol other unspecified (ethyl)

Gruenewald & Ponicki, 1995a), and between cirrhosis mortality rates and general socioeconomic factors at the national level (Holder & Parker, 1992), focused studies of these outcomes at lower levels of aggregation generally have not been attempted. A singular attempt by Watts and Rabow (1983) suggests, however, that such analyses on a city-by-city basis (with city sizes ranging down to 10,000) are feasible. Furthermore, when restricting analyses to communities of 40,000 or more and aggregating across all sources of alcohol- or drug-related mortality, analytic techniques appropriate to low base-rate data may prove adequate to the task of studying these sources of mortality between communities.[2]

Table 4.4
Mortality Due to Drug Abuse (ICD-9-CM)

Code		Definition
304		Drug dependence
	304.0	Opioids (heroin, meperidine, methadone, morphine, opium)
	304.1	Barbiturates
	304.2	Cocaine
	304.3	Cannabis
	304.4	Amphetamine
	304.5	Hallucinogen
	304.6	Other
	304.7	Combinations within opioids
	304.8	Combination outside opioids
	304.9	Unspecified drug dependence
305		Nondependent use of drugs
	305.2	Cannabis abuse
	305.3	Hallucinogen abuse
	305.4	Barbiturate abuse
	305.5	Opioid abuse
	305.6	Cocaine abuse
	305.7	Amphetamine abuse
E850.0		Accidental poisoning, heroin
E850.1		Accidental poisoning, methadone
E850.2		Accidental poisoning, other opiates
E851		Accidental poisoning, barbiturates
E853		Accidental poisoning, tranquilizers
E854		Accidental poisoning, psychotropics
	E854.0	Antidepressants
	E854.1	Psychodysleptics (hallucinogens)
	E854.2	Psychostimulants

Finally, although largely unexplored, morbidity data available from hospital discharge indexes may prove to be a valuable source of information regarding alcohol and drug-related problems within communities. Depending on reporting procedures, these data may or may not be collected at a patient-specific level, causing counted rates of discharge to be inflated by repeat users of hospital facilities. Like mortality data, however, primary diagnostic categories are coded using the International

Classification of Diseases scheme, and, for some states, alcohol- or drug-related discharge data may be specifically noted. The organization and specification of these data, however, are state specific, potentially causing problems in establishing the comparability of data sources between states. Additionally, major changes in admitting and discharge practices that have occurred over the past decade have lowered discharge counts and average length of hospital stays.

All the health data sources discussed provide information aggregated at a remarkable degree of geographic specificity. So, for example, traffic crash data (both fatal and nonfatal) can be located by cross streets within communities (Gruenewald, Millar, & Treno, 1993) and, thus, located within any arbitrary geographic unit, making these data completely compatible with all community definitions. Death certificate data very often include the zip code of the residence of the decedent, and certainly the zip code of the reporting facility, allowing reasonably precise characterizations of locations within communities. Perhaps the least specific of the sources is hospital discharge data, which provides either a three-digit zip code (the first three digits) for individuals discharged in the client-based reporting system or the full zip code in the event-based reporting system.

The temporal specificity of these indicators is also quite exceptional. Traditionally, traffic crash data have been coded by the date and time of accident, allowing aggregation to any temporal unit of analysis. Mortality data and hospital discharge data, although typically made available on an annual basis, contain information about date of death and discharge, respectively.

Applications

Of the indicators listed in Table 4.2, those related to traffic crashes have been the most thoroughly investigated. A number of large-scale time series analyses of data on single-vehicle crashes have been performed at the state level. These studies have related changes in measures of crash rates over time to changes in alcohol availability (Blose & Holder, 1987), laws regarding server liability (Wagenaar & Holder, 1991), and the minimum drinking age (Wagenaar, 1986a, 1986b). These studies have been more recently supplemented by examinations of single-vehicle fatalities in both cross-sectional (Saffer & Grossman, 1987) and time series cross-sectional (Gruenewald & Ponicki, 1995b) data sets. At these levels of aggregation, alcohol-related crash measures have demonstrated considerable utility. At lower levels of aggregation, however, information on the performance of crash measures is scant. Methodologically rigorous community-level studies of single-vehicle crashes are just being beginning. Gruenewald, Millar, Treno, Yang, Ponicki, & Roeper (1996) demonstrate that traffic crash data can be analyzable at the community level, but that these analyses require some additional consideration of the spatial geography of the community.

A similar, but more severe, situation arises in the analysis of other mortality data. For example, although the feasibility of national (Holder & Parker, 1992) and state-level (Gruenewald & Ponicki, 1995a) studies of cirrhosis mortality rates have been demonstrated, there is but one demonstration of the feasibility of studying this outcome at a community level (Watts & Rabow, 1983). Studies of other less frequent forms of alcohol and drug-related mortality and morbidity appear nonexistent.

Schools

Given the number of school-based alcohol and drug studies (Moskowitz, 1989) and the enormous size of survey research efforts directed at understanding alcohol and drug abuse among school-age children (Johnston et al., 1992), one would think that extensive indicator data would be regularly collected on this population. Surprisingly, not only is little data collected, but little of what is collected is of much use to researchers interested in drug and alcohol abuse among young people. We have been unable to uncover any consistently collected archival data from school systems that shed light on either drug or alcohol use or abuse or school-based problems related to substance abuse.

Available school data characterize the demographics of the school population (e.g., age, gender, ethnic group), enrollment levels, and, frequently, some measure of achievement. As shown in Table 4.5, only two of these measures appear consistently enough across communities in the United States to justify regular examination—measures of school achievement and enrollment levels.

Remarkably, meaningful measures of school drop-out rates are particularly difficult to obtain. Because on any given day, a substantial minority of the student population is absent from school (estimated to run about 20% in California), classification of students into drop-out status represents an ambiguous process at best. This fact, combined with the fiscal tie of enrollment rates to funding levels in most school districts, tends to undermine the interpretability of drop-out data. For this reason, the most sensible figure to obtain regarding school populations is the

Table 4.5

Indicators of Schools and the Economy

Area	Indicator	Expected Geographic Specificity	Expected Periodicity	Example Source
Schools	Achievement	School districts	Annually	California Department of Education/school district administrative offices
	Enrollment	School districts	Annually	California Department of Education/school district administrative offices
Economy	Alcohol availability (outlet locations)	Street level/ zip/county	Daily/ annually	California Department of Alcohol Beverage Control
	Retail alcohol prices	City/state	Quarterly	American Chamber of Commerce Research Association
	Consumer Price Index	Region/ state/city	Quarterly/ annually	Department of Commerce
	Retail activity	State/county	Annually	County business patterns
	NPA Data Services Employment and Income Trends	County	Annually	NPA Data Services

enrollment level. This number records the expectations of schools with regard to their assigned student populations and, relative to definitions of drop-outs, is clearly operationalized.

Geographic and Temporal Specificity

Most school-based data are geographically quite specific, relating to particular school districts within communities. The temporal availability of these data, however, varies considerably as a function of content and reporting format. Although attendance data are tracked, in principle, on a daily basis, these data may be compiled only on a semester or quarter basis, at best, and often not in electronic form. Annual compilations of attendance information are most often available and, in the case of achievement tests, only annual compilations of these data may be obtained.

Economy

A number of indicators related to local community economies can be used to index access to and the use of alcoholic beverages. As shown in Table 4.5, these include alcohol availability (outlet locations), retail alcohol beverage prices, measures of rates of inflation (Consumer Price Index), and indexes of local economic health (retail activity). These particular indicators represent a specific subset of broader economic indicators typically available on a national and state basis from a variety of sources. Thus, the last resource listed in Table 4.5, NPA Data Services Employment and Income Trends (Terleckyj & Coleman, 1992a), presents a compendium of information on employment and income available at the county level. The value of these data sources is discussed separately below. Because of the inevitable paucity of information on the economics of the illegal drug market (e.g., Reuter, 1992), available economic indicators may be only tangentially related to market activities in this arena.[3]

The availability of alcoholic beverages is most frequently tracked by state alcohol beverage control (ABC) agencies whose role (since the end of Prohibition in 1933) in each state has been to protect the public welfare in regulating alcohol beverage distribution (Janes & Gruenewald, 1991). ABC data provide the community researcher with excellent sources for identifying areas of great outlet concentrations within communities (Gruenewald, Millar, & Treno, 1993).

The quality of data maintained by state ABCs is generally quite high. There is extreme variation from state to state, however, with the majority of states able to provide detailed lists of licensees (e.g., California) and a small minority of states maintaining and providing little to no information about either licensees or premise locations (e.g., Nevada). The geographic specificity of ABC data is generally quite good, with individual street addresses supplied in most cases. The expected periodicity of these measures is also quite good, with annual data common and daily data available occasionally. Because daily data often constitute little more than daily records of license renewals, however, the precision of these measures is subject to some skepticism. Delays in receiving and processing renewals, determinations of failures to renew, and so on all introduce delays into the processing of these data, reducing their temporal precision. Measures of retail alcohol beverage prices have been notoriously difficult to obtain, even at the state level. For this reason, many economic researchers have resorted to surrogates for beverage prices in the form of excise tax rates (available for only a subset of states, see Cook & Tauchen, 1982; Gruenewald, Ponicki, & Holder, 1993). The small percentage of variance in alcohol beverage prices accounted for by excise taxes, however, argues for the use of price data whenever available (e.g., Nelson, 1988).[4]

More recently, some consideration has been given to using measures of alcohol beverage prices available from a cost of living survey operated by the American Chamber of Commerce Research Association (ACCRA; 1987). These data are obtained and tracked by ACCRA on a quarterly basis for several hundred communities and cities in the United States.[5]

The Consumer Price Index (CPI) is a standard economic indicator familiar to most residents of the United States. It should also be familiar to all researchers interested in the economics of alcohol and drug use. This index has been used to summarize changes in the relative prices of a broad spectrum of commodities over the past 30 years or more. It is introduced here as an important indicator of the general economic conditions in which the markets for alcohol and drugs operate. As has been noted by many researchers (most recently by Moore & Cook, 1991), although nominal prices for alcoholic beverages (prices charged at retail markets) have increased over past years, "real" prices for these beverages (adjusted for rates of inflation) have declined almost continuously since 1967. The retail prices of drugs fluctuate, but changes in drug prices must be evaluated within the context of the overall consumer marketplace. Additionally, there are CPIs for beer, wine, and spirits.

General measures of retail activity, particularly employment levels and rates of openings and closings of businesses, are often a good index of local economic growth and decline (see Gruenewald, Ponicki, & Holder, 1993; Wagenaar & Streff, 1989). These data are available on an annual basis at the state and county level through *County Business Patterns,* an annual publication of the Department of Commerce. The minimum level of aggregation available from this source is the county, and within counties information is sometimes withheld to protect business confidentiality. Thus, the temporal and geographic resolutions of these data are not as precise as ideally desired, but suitable to establishing general local economic conditions—conditions that have been shown, among other things, to correlate with changes in measures of the physical availability of alcohol over time (Gruenewald, Ponicki, & Holder, 1993).

As noted above, the last resource listed in Table 4.5, NPA Data Services Employment and Income Trends (Terleckyj & Coleman, 1992a), presents a compendium of information on employment and income available at the county level. This is one source for a variety of economic measures based on extrapolations and interpolations of data available from branches of the Department of Commerce. In the case of employment and income trends, NPA data provide estimates of economic measures at the county level adjusted for changes in demographic and business compositions of local areas. The estimation procedures include models that account for in- and out-migration by demographic groups during intercensal years (years between the decennial census). Examples of available data from this source are (1) numbers of business proprietors, employment, and industry earnings, by industry sector (compiled from the Bureau of Labor Statistics and National Income and Product Accounts); (2) personal income; and (3) real income adjusted by the Personal Consumption Expenditure Deflator (from the Bureau of Economic Analysis of the Department of Commerce).

Applications

Most of the indicators discussed here have been used historically by economists in studies of alcohol problems in the United States (for reviews, see Chaloupka, 1993; Cook & Moore, 1991; Grossman, 1991; Leung & Phelps, 1991). These studies have almost exclusively focused on national or state geographic units, rarely considering smaller levels of aggregation or analyses of individual data (cf. Coate & Grossman, 1988). Entry of economic factors into more broadly specified models of alcohol problems has been a rather recent phenomenon in alcohol studies, one that has allowed a comparison of the relative effects of economic versus other factors on alcohol problems (e.g., physical availability, Gruenewald, Ponicki, & Holder, 1993; and other routine life activities, Treno, Parker, & Holder, 1993). These studies have tended to suggest that the role of economic factors in the explanation of alcohol use is rather small relative to other environmental and social conditions.

Studies of drug problems from an economic perspective have been few in number and have tended to be restricted to considerations of the global economics of the drug trade (Reuter, 1992) or to economic models of local conditions of drug availability (Moore, 1990). Obviously, the

absence of much economic data on the illegal drug market has prohib-
ited further explorations. Some recent publications have included an
economic study of the effect of marijuana decriminalization on emergency room admissions using DAWN data (available from a small
subset of urban areas, Model, 1993) and a study of drug pricing using
data available from the Western States Information Network (Caulkins
& Padman, 1993).

In the current context, these studies are more notable for the credence
they place in their indicators of drug problems and prices than for their
presumed analytic outcomes. To accept the outcomes of Model's (1993)
analyses, one must presume that self-reports of marijuana use and
physicians' screening of such use will remain unaffected by decriminalization (both serious measurement problems in emergency room
data, Treno, Cooper, & Roeper, 1994). To accept the price figures of
Caulkins and Padman's (1993) study, one must assume that prices, or
price ranges, obtained by enforcement agents on undercover "buys" (a
selection bias problem in itself) accurately index prices in the illegal
market. This, of course, would be the case only in a market with narrow
price ranges and low price volatility.

Remarking at this point on the absence of data regarding activities in
the illegal drug market, it is important to note a similar lack of some
important data in the legal market for alcohol. One indicator notably
absent from the list presented in Table 4.5 is some measure of alcohol
sales. The primary reason for the concentration of studies of alcohol
problems on state-level data is that sales data are available only at this
level (e.g., Gruenewald, Ponicki, & Holder, 1993). Alcohol sales measures based on tax receipts and wholesale distributions (1) only indirectly
reflect retail activity, (2) are differentiated by product (e.g., beer, wine,
and spirits) but not brand type, and (3) likely reflect stocking practices
of retail establishments. The absence of alcohol sales data at the local
level forces community researchers to seek elsewhere for other measures of use.

Demographics

Substantial demographic data by census tract are available from the
U.S. Bureau of the Census on a decennial basis (Table 4.6). These data
include the age, gender, racial, and ethnic compositions of local populations, household composition (distributions of adults and youth),
religious preferences, marital status, estimates of household income, in-
and out-migration, and a number of other measures. In addition, the

Table 4.6

Indicators of Demographics and Politics

Area	Indicator	Expected Geographic Specificity	Expected Periodicity	Example Source
Demographics	Population data	Census tracts/ zip code/county	Decennially	U.S. Census
	NPA Data Services household and demographic data	County	Annually	NPA Data Services
Politics	Percentage eligible persons voting	Congressional district/state	Voting years	Congressional Quarterly/League of Women Voters
	Percentage registered voters voting	Congressional district/state	Voting years	Congressional Quarterly/League of Women Voters

census's *Current Population Reports* serve as a valuable adjunct, presenting annual updates on a number of measures (e.g., age, gender, and race distributions). These updates, however, are often available only for geographic units of some size (e.g., states, metropolitan areas, and, sometimes, counties).

To provide more complete estimates of population characteristics for smaller geographic areas, a number of private companies use census data as a base from which to project local area characteristics. As noted in Table 4.6, NPA Data Services provides some demographic information annually on a county-by-county basis. Demographic characteristics of county areas are continuously updated and reestimated based on data from the census and other sources in the Department of Commerce, taking into account expected rates of in- and out-migration (Terleckyj & Coleman, 1992b). Thus, NPA provides estimates of gender, race, and age by income groups and numbers of households by county.

Applications

Given the wide disparity of alcohol and drug consumption patterns among demographic groups (Clark & Hilton, 1991; Johnston et al.,

1992; National Institute for Drug Abuse, 1991), indicators of population demographic composition are essential covariates in models of community substance abuse. Failure to include these covariates generally results in overestimates of the efficacy of preventive interventions (e.g., Grossman, 1991; Leung & Phelps, 1991; Moore & Cook, 1991). Thus, for example, the effects of changes in alcohol taxes and prices on alcohol sales are likely overstated, as are the effects of other prevention strategies due to the failures of most studies to account for the covarying effects of changes in population composition (e.g., age-gender cohorts, Treno, Parker, & Holder, 1993; religious preferences and urbanicity, Gruenewald, Ponicki, & Holder, 1993) or other features of the environment—for example, the physical availability of alcohol and drugs (Gruenewald, Ponicki, & Holder, 1993; Moore, 1990).

Comparisons of the results of various studies strongly argue that, contrary to arguments commonly found in the economics literature, demographic characteristics of populations change substantially over time and are a source of both cross-sectional and longitudinal variation in alcohol and drug use. One would expect this to be the case particularly in small communities where in- and out-migration may dramatically alter population composition in relatively short spans of time. Time series of community-based data of the sort necessary to establish the effect of changes in demographic characteristics on drug and alcohol use at the community level have not been adequately developed thus far (cf. Gruenewald, Hill, Treno, & Taff, 1993; Holder, Grube, Gruenewald, Saltz, Treno, & Voas, 1995). The state- and national-level studies presented above, however, suggest that there is more volatility in demographic variables than previously expected.

Politics

Archival indicators of political activity may be particularly valuable as indexes of the involvement of local populations in the political process. Insofar as community involvement is one goal of many current alcohol and drug initiatives, indicators of such involvement may provide important process-level information concerning the extent to which citizen action is catalyzed.

Two indicators of political activity are presented in Table 4.6—percentage of eligible persons voting and percentage of registered voters voting. These appear to be the only relevant indicators of political participation that are currently reported on a regular basis at a sufficient level of geographic specificity. These indicators measure voter participation in elections in terms of eligibility and registration, respectively, and can be used as surrogates of public participation in local political processes.

Although geographically precise with respect to community definitions (many communities' boundaries are concurrent with congressional districts), these indicators are collected only during voting years. And, because voter participation varies strongly as a function of type of election (local, congressional, senate, and presidential), temporal variation in these measures may not reflect variations in local political involvement per se, but rather local interest generated in larger state and national races.

Despite these problems, measures of voter behavior probably provide a reasonably accurate reflection of cross-sectional differences in political participation and, due to the lack of alternative data sources, are likely to be the best local indicators available of participation in the political process.

SUMMARY

This chapter presents a general summary of currently available local data in the areas of crime, health, education, the economy, demographics, and politics—all areas that must be considered in the examination of alcohol and other drug-related issues from a systems perspective. In our review of these data, we have issued a number of warnings. Community-generated data are, as implied by the systems perspective discussed above, produced for reasons unrelated to research needs. Thus, they must not be taken at face value, but rather must be critically scrutinized. Additionally, they should, when possible, be supported by other data. Given this premise, it is appropriate to consider the extent to which other, nonarchival, data can be used to supplement archival data. In the next chapter, we consider this issue by exploring the use of survey data as supplements to archival data.

NOTES

1. One notable gap in Table 4.2 is the absence of measures of mortality and morbidity related to drownings, burns, and falls (Saltz, Gruenewald, & Hennessy, 1992). Although current research suggests that alcohol involvement in these events is considerable, the

availability of appropriate indicators of source of trauma (namely, event codes related to these occurrences) is limited. Treno, Cooper, and Roeper (1994) are currently investigating the availability and utility of measures of nonvehicular traumatic events related to alcohol.

2. In particular, Poisson and negative binomial regression models be applied to such data (Greene, 1993). This has not been the approach taken by any of the authors cited here.

3. A necessary and important argument is to be made that many, if not all, of the features of the alcohol market are reflected in the market for illegal drugs (Caulkins & Padman, 1993; Preble & Casey, 1969). The exigencies of supply and demand are to be met in both economies. Thus, as should be expected, demand functions for illegal drugs will include measures of personal income, drug prices, physical availability, and so on. Supply functions will include production, importation, and measures of distribution flow. Because in the illegal drug market the community systems that would normally produce indicator data are almost all illegal, however, no reliable indicator data will generally be forthcoming.

4. Tax rates may be of interest to policy researchers as a form of preventive intervention.

5. The relatively small geographic variation to be found in beverage prices (particularly relative to the broad spectrum of market prices for alcohol, Treno, Nephew, Ponicki, & Gruenewald, 1993), suggests that indexes from nearby communities may do well for communities in which such data are not available. This ability to use alcohol price data from nearby communities is a special case, however, and should not be generalized to other indicators discussed in this book.

5

Community Indicators and Survey Data

Within the limitations outlined in the previous chapters, community indicators can provide useful measures of drug- and alcohol-related problems (e.g., alcohol-related crashes and drug poisonings) and community activities related to the prevention of drug and alcohol abuse (e.g., crime enforcement and the provision of treatment services). These limitations are, however, considerable, and the ill-considered use of indicators can lead to the appearance of change where none exists and the failure to detect change where real change occurs.

The validity of measurement in the social sciences—especially social science field research—has long been questioned (for discussion of validity as a methodological issue, see Carmines & Zellner, 1979). Although social scientists are constantly striving to improve measurement accuracy, it is also recognized that there may be inherent problems in the measurement of complex behavioral, social, and organizational phenomena. More than 20 years ago, this recognition led social scientists to propose a multimeasure approach in which different measures of the same phenomenon are used to increase confidence in observed results.

Two broad classes of data are available to community researchers. One is the community indicator data discussed in this monograph. The other is data available from surveys conducted within communities on an ongoing basis. This chapter discusses the strengths and weaknesses of survey data and the ways in which indicators and surveys may be used in concert to increase the richness and validity of community alcohol and other drug research.

OVERVIEW OF COMMUNITY
SURVEY DATA COLLECTION

Within the context of community research, relevant types of community surveys include continuous or periodic data collection from general

55

community populations (e.g., surveys of adults, Holder et al., 1995; surveys of both adults and youth, Gruenewald, Hill, Treno, & Taff, 1993) and focus on special populations (e.g., school-based surveys of school children and roadside surveys of drivers, Holder et al., 1995). Data may be collected using direct interviews of individuals, mail surveys, paper-and-pencil surveys in group situations (e.g., classrooms), or random-digit dial telephone interview techniques. Sample units may consist of individuals within households or individuals within schools and classrooms (or other units such as workplaces and roadside checkpoints).

Like indicator data, survey data have limitations that must be recognized. Perhaps the paramount limitation is the relatively small number of content areas any one survey can address. The constraints of fielding a survey (e.g., in terms of time, energy, and budgets) limit the breadth of any survey considerably. Thus, the contents of survey instruments must be focused, specific, and selected with great forethought given to the outcomes of concern. Generally, survey researchers find themselves eliminating more variables than they retain by the time a survey is actually fielded.

The validity of surveys is highly dependent on sampling, because it is almost never the case that all eligible respondents are surveyed. Sampling bias may arise from the failure to obtain a representative sample of the studied population across all eligible units (e.g., individuals within households and households within communities). Self-selection bias may arise if the characteristics of individuals who refuse to participate in the survey are systematically related to sampling strata, person characteristics, or outcome measures (e.g., if heavy drug users are more likely to refuse to participate in a survey on drugs than light users or nonusers).

Instrumentation bias may arise through the use of poorly specified measurement instruments (e.g., through the use of improperly constructed measures of alcohol consumption, Gruenewald & Nephew, 1994). Memory effects may result in forgetting bias through the inability of some respondents to recall information requested on surveys (e.g., "On how many days in the past 4 weeks have you had one or more full drinks of alcohol?"). Finally, respondents' reluctance to report illicit behaviors (e.g., "Have you used a needle for the injection of any illegal drug in the past 6 months?") may lead to self-report response bias.

Despite their limitations, survey data provide a source of complementary information essential to supporting the valid use of indicator data.

INDICATORS AND SURVEY DATA

Community indicator data and community survey data reflect very different levels of analysis and tap into very different community processes. Thus, they are fundamentally different from each other. Community indicator data are generated by functioning community systems. Thus, law enforcement agencies produce data on arrests, educational institutions produce data on achievement of those educated, economic systems produce data on production and sales, and health care systems produce data on rates of observed morbidity and mortality and treatment admissions or discharges. By contrast, survey research data provide information on the activities and views of individuals within communities that often would not otherwise be observable—for example, peer influences on drug and alcohol use, public opinions, victimization rates, and potentially dangerous behaviors related to drinking and drug use, such as intoxicated driving.

Taken alone, neither community indicators nor surveys provide a very complete picture of the community. When combined, however, they provide a relatively comprehensive basis on which to analyze community systems and evaluate community programs. As shown in Figure 5.1, in fact, the two sources of information can be viewed as complementary in a number of respects. This figure displays some sample indicators available from communities (on the left) and some complementary self-report measures often used in community surveys of substance-abuse-related problems (on the right). A review of Figure 5.1 provides a sense of the ways in which indicator and survey data can be intertwined to support one another. Discussions of the complementary nature of indicators and surveys follow for the areas discussed in Chapter 4 (crime, health, schools, economic measures, demographics, and political activity).

Crime

Consider the two crime indicators in Figure 5.1—drunk driving arrests and drug sales and possessions arrests. Surveys can supplement these arrest figures with self-reports of drunk driving incidence and prevalence, alcohol use, drug use, rates of criminal victimization related to drug sales, and reports of neighborhood drug sales (e.g., "In the past 6 months have you been approached for drug sales within 3 blocks of

Archival Community Indicators	General Population Survey Items
Crime	
Drunk driving arrests	Self-reports of drunk driving incidence and prevalence Self-reports of alcohol use
Drug sales and possession arrests	Reports of neighborhood drug sales Self-reports of drug use Rates of criminal victimization
Health	
Mortality due to alcohol abuse	Self-reports of alcohol use chronicity and severity Self-reports of alcohol dependence and problems
Alcohol and drug treatment services	Self-reports of health care utilization
Schools	
Enrollment	Self-reports of school drop-outs and attendance
Economy	
Alcohol availability (outlet locations)	Self-reports of physical, social, and subjective availability
(Drug availability)	Self-reports of physical, social, and subjective availability
Retail activity	( )
Demographics	
Gender, race, ethnicity, household composition, etc.	Gender, race, ethnicity, household composition, etc.
Politics	
Percentage registered voters voting	( )
( )	Public opinions and political issues

Figure 5.1. Complementary Community Monitoring Systems

your home?"). One source for our knowledge of the comparatively limited effect of arrests on the total mass of drunk driving events is comparisons of arrest rates and self-reports (Perrine et al., 1989). Similarly, arrest rates for drug sales and possession can be compared to self- (or friends') reports of drug use and evidence of drug sales within neighborhood areas. Using both sources of data, disjunctures between arrest events and criminal events can be explored and the interrelationships between police and criminal activity that result in arrests can be studied.

Health

Health indicators tend to be restricted to measures of morbidity and mortality outcomes or service utilization. As shown in Figure 5.1, these health indicators can be complemented by self-reports of chronicity and severity of alcohol and drug use (e.g., measures of "heavy" drinking, Clark & Hilton, 1991; measures of frequent drug use, Johnson et al., 1990). They may also be supplemented by survey measures of drug and alcohol dependence (e.g., the alcohol dependency scale, Skinner & Allen, 1982) and self-reports of health care utilization (Gruenewald, Hill, et al., 1993). Thus, structural relationships between consumption patterns and health outcomes—for example, between patterns of alcohol use and problems related to dependence (Gruenewald, 1991)—and relationships between the characteristics of those who seek treatment (using survey data) and treatment services provided (using archival indicators) can be explored.

A particular advantage of survey research in exploring health outcomes is that events (e.g., injuries related to alcohol and other drug use, Holder, et al., 1995) can be detected that do not result in admission to a medical facility. Thus, survey data can detect relationships between substance use and problems that may be precursors to the detectable events (e.g., hospitalizations for treatment) indexed by indicator data.

Schools

School enrollment data can be supplemented by estimates of self-reported rates of dropping out of school by school-age young people. Surveys of youth conducted outside of schools are particularly valuable in this regard (Gruenewald, Hill, et al., 1993).

Economic Measures

Measures of the physical availability of alcohol (e.g., as usually given by license counts from state alcohol beverage control agencies) can be supplemented by survey measures of the perceived physical availability of alcohol (e.g., "Is there an alcohol outlet within 3 blocks of your home?"), the social availability of alcohol (e.g., "Is alcohol generally served at parties and other gatherings that you attend?"), and the subjective availability of alcohol (e.g., "How willing are you to make separate shopping trips for alcohol").[1] Of course, self-report measures of this kind are likely to be subject to substantial irrelevant variation due to the drinking patterns of consumers and purchasers, making their validity unknown (Gruenewald, 1994).

The availability of illegal drugs, as indicated in Figure 5.1, is not ascertainable using any widely published community indicator or set of indicators. Although it is to be expected that police actions will be focused on areas in which such availability is greatest, and, therefore, presumably the police are cognizant of the relative availability of illegal drugs, detailed records of police actions are seldom kept in retrievable form and may bear a stronger correlation to the visibility of drug sales than to the availability of illegal drugs per se (Kleiman & Smith, 1990). Thus, the community researcher's only resort is to self-report data of one kind or another. These data may come from reports of users who are entering or currently participating in treatment (see studies reviewed in Hunt, 1990) or from reports of community members concerning local drug activities (Gruenewald, Hill, et al., 1993). In both these cases, however, bias is likely—from limited access to a broad population of users or limited access to knowledgeable community members.

Occasionally, a survey study of the alcohol market appears in the research literature (e.g., Treno, Nephew, Ponicki, & Gruenewald, 1993). These surveys, however, have been rather narrowly focused and do not provide general information on the economic state of the alcohol market (e.g., local production, wholesale distribution, wholesale and retail prices, beverage sales by establishment). Other surveys of local market activity also take place sporadically in some communities based on local market survey demands; however, such surveys are not administered with an eye to survey replication, but rather with an eye to market investment (e.g., determining advertising spread, retail store locations, and so on).

Demographics

Demographic characteristics of community populations are available from the U.S. Census Bureau. These data are survey data and subject, therefore, to all the criticisms of surveys noted above. They become available to communities only after compilation (and projection) by the federal government, however, providing an achieved status similar to other indicators. Census data can be complemented by data obtained from community surveys. Local survey data may be of great value in determining demographic features unique to the local population (e.g., ethnic and racial categories not addressed in the census). Such data may also be particularly useful if the local population is subject to considerable in- and out-migration (e.g., in broader communities with large numbers of seasonal migrants), or if a large proportion of the population is undocumented.

Political Activity

Counts of the percentage of registered voters voting, despite the weaknesses cited in Chapter 4, remain the best indicator of local political participation. Also of use may be the ways citizens vote on important ballot issues. Many, if not most, issues related to alcohol and drugs are missed by these measures, however. Thus, surveys can explore the opinions of individuals (voters or not) on particular political and local community issues. Such data can be a valuable source for guiding the activities of local community groups and informing researchers of the foci of local community concerns (see Holder et al., 1995).

Example

The complementary nature of indicators and surveys may be illustrated by considering potential relationships between measures of impoverishment and measures of alcohol and other drug use and resulting problems. Indicator data might be particularly appropriate for the investigation of the dynamic relationships between measures of impoverishment (e.g., income and unemployment) and measures of alcohol and drug problems (e.g., alcohol and drug treatment discharges). Over long periods of time (say, 30 years), the temporal dynamics of impoverishment could be used to predict changes in alcohol and drug problems.

Because population surveys are rarely administered on an ongoing basis over a sufficient number of years to perform similar analyses, indicator data may be the only way to explore the temporal dynamics of this relationship.

Should such a relationship be observed, however, it might be argued that the relationship between impoverishment and the particular measures of alcohol and drug problems used (e.g., alcohol and drug treatment discharges) does not reflect the effects of impoverishment on drug and alcohol use per se, but rather the effects of impoverishment on treatment-seeking behavior. In this case, only survey-based measures can be used to explicate this more detailed conceptual issue. The community researcher could gain some understanding of this issue by measuring drug and alcohol use levels for a period of time across a number of geographic units, then relating these measurements to indicator data for the same period. If usage levels correlated well with drug and alcohol treatment discharges, then it is likely that the long-term measurement of such behaviors reflects actual use and general problem levels—not only, or especially, treatment-seeking behaviors per se.

THE INTERRELATIONSHIP BETWEEN THE BEHAVIOR OF COMMUNITY SYSTEMS AND INDIVIDUALS

Indicators index the activities of the community systems that generate them, whereas surveys index the attitudes, beliefs, and behaviors of individuals. Insofar as both individual characteristics and the activities of community systems jointly determine alcohol and drug consumption and related problems, both must be considered and both must be measured to understand alcohol and other drug (AOD) problems in a given community.

Two examples that illustrate this point can be drawn from a study of a community intervention funded by the Robert Wood Johnson Foundation (Fighting Back) in 21 sites in the United States. The intervention was intended to affect community systems addressing drug and alcohol problems in many ways. Specific interventions included community efforts to reduce the availability of alcohol through changes in zoning law, "erase and replace" campaigns to eliminate alcohol and tobacco billboards, and Friday night basketball programs to provide alternatives

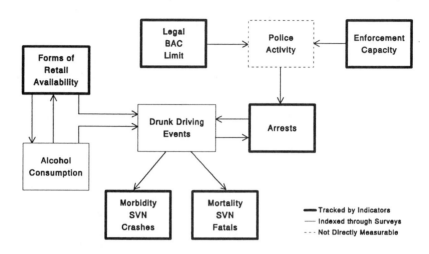

Figure 5.2. Law Enforcement Activities and Drunk Driving Events

for youths. Given the view that solutions to AOD problems required community sensitive approaches, the local Fighting Back staffs were given considerable latitude in intervention focus. Thus, in one Southwestern community where alcohol is the source of most major social problems, a major focus was on reduction of alcohol availability. In one Northeastern community where cocaine was the major source of problems, this substance was targeted. In all cases, however, the goal was a reduction or substantial alteration of problems related to drugs and alcohol, including drunk driving, illegal drug sales, and other crimes associated with drinking and illegal drug use. Figures 5.2 and 5.3 provide conceptual outlines of the interrelationships of some of the community systems and individual characteristics relevant to two outcomes of general concern to many of the Fighting Back interventions and subsequent evaluation—drunk driving (Figure 5.2) and the sales and use of illegal drugs (Figure 5.3). Outlined in both figures are community systems activity that may be tracked by indicators (bold boxes), individual behaviors that may be indexed through surveys (unbolded boxes), and important aspects of community systems activity that are not directly measurable but may sometimes be inferred (dashed boxes).

Figure 5.2 presents a brief conceptual outline of the interactions of the community systems and individual characteristics related to drunk

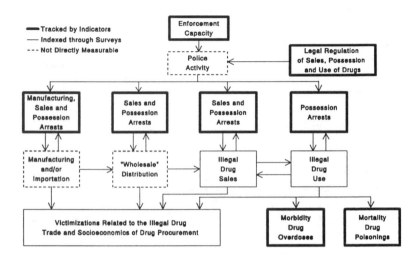

Figure 5.3. Law Enforcement Activities and Drug Sales and Use Events

driving events. Retail availability of alcohol and alcohol consumption (i.e., demand) interact to produce drunk driving events. These drunk driving events are legally proscribed by a blood alcohol limit established in law (the upper box), which influences the activities of police (box to upper right); may result in death or injury to the driver, occupants of his or her vehicle, or others (the lower two boxes); or may result in arrest by the police (box to the right). Arrest events themselves may suppress drunk driving activity (through the specific and general deterrence of these acts) and are increased by any increase in drunk driving due to other sources (e.g., increased drinking). Arrests are, furthermore, a function of police activity (upper dashed box). Should the police choose to enforce drunk driving laws aggressively, drunk driving arrests will increase. Finally, police activity itself is conditional on available resources for enforcement—enforcement capacity (box to the upper right).[2]

All but one of the variables in Figure 5.2 can be indexed by either a community indicator or a measure available from general population community surveys. It is a testament to the wide public concern with alcohol use and drunk driving, and the political responsiveness to this concern, that so many data relevant to this problem are available from archival sources. Thus, a number of community systems provide indicators relevant to drinking and driving activities. The law enforcement system provides data on the legal codes of restraint, some measures of enforcement capacity, and estimates of drunk driving arrests. The alcohol beverage control system provides data on legal outlets for beverage distribution, and state and national reporting systems provide data on crashes. The one area in which no direct information is available is specific police activity with respect to the enforcement of drunk driving laws. Consequently, some measure of enforcement capacity is necessary as a surrogate for these activities.

Sales and use of illegal drugs are, by definition, illegal. This observation, however obvious and tautological, captures the central problem in analyzing community systems related to illegal substance use. Specifically, the market for illegal drugs is—and desires to be—invisible to the police while remaining visible to consumers. Thus, sales and use of illegal drugs, like most consensual crimes (e.g., prostitution, Hunt, 1990), are largely invisible activities not indexed by any of the usual measures of legal markets.

The invisibility of much of the activity related to the manufacture and distribution of illegal drugs is reflected in Figure 5.3. Activities related to the manufacturing or importation and "wholesale" distribution of illegal drugs are directly measurable by neither any available community indicator nor any feasible survey research measure. Although these activities may lead to observable rates of arrest (the string of bold boxes across the center of the figure) and to rates of victimization measurable on victimization surveys (box at the lower left), the activities cannot be directly observed through routinely collected measures. Illegal drug activities only begin to achieve visibility as they appear in response to survey items regarding the sale of drugs (e.g., "Have you seen evidence of illegal drug sales in your neighborhood in the past 6 months?"), drug use, or drug-related victimizations (e.g., elevated reported levels of property crime victimizations). The effects of drug use appear in community indicators only in the form of the fatal and nonfatal sequelae of illegal use (e.g., drug poisonings and overdoses) or in the form of increased drug treatment activity (not shown in the figure).

Illegal drug use is not only invisible, it is rare. The low incidence of illegal drug use further limits the use of indicators in its measurement. Take, for example, use among adolescents and young adults. In the case of alcohol, the major problem related to use in this age group—fatal and nonfatal traffic crashes—can be and is directly measured. Changes in fatal and nonfatal crashes may be directly linked to changes in patterns of consumption. By contrast, illicit drug use and its sequelae are sufficiently rare among adolescents and young adults that no analogue to fatal crashes has been identified. Moreover, measures that are available are related to very heavy levels of consumption (i.e., poisonings, over-doses, and problems that presumably lead to treatment) rarely seen among adolescents and young adults. These measures are insensitive, at least in the short run, to interventions intended to affect the drug use behaviors of young people. Thus, the only currently available option for indexing patterns of consumption is surveys.

Clearly, in the case of illegal drug activity, components of the com-munity system are invisible to both the analysis of community indica-tors and survey research data. It is doubtful whether any other method could adequately index these components at the community level. Despite these limitations, however, Figure 5.3 demonstrates that illegal drug use is researchable at the community level. The violence and intimidation associated directly with the illegal drug trade, and property crimes related to use, may be indexed by survey data on criminal victimization. Arrest data will reflect to some extent the growth and decline of illegal drug markets. Finally, sales of illegal drugs and demand for drugs can be indexed from survey data. Although the case is not as clear-cut as it is for drunk driving, Figure 5.3 demonstrates the feasibil-ity of analyzing a variety of community outcomes related to illicit drugs through the complementary use of indicators and community surveys.

SUMMARY

Community indicators and survey-based measures may be used in a complementary manner to inform researchers about changes in the community environment, specific community systems, and individual attitudes, beliefs, and behaviors. Relying on the strengths of the two measurement approaches, complementary pairings of data sources can provide cross-validations of measured changes and deeper insights into the workings of community systems and the behaviors of individuals who participate in them.

NOTES

1. The literature dealing with the measurement of availability using survey methods is best accessed through the key publications of Rabow, Schwartz, Stevens, and Watts (1982) and Smart (1980). Abbey, Scott, and Smith (1993) present a recent summary of

this work. Yet, despite the wide use of this approach to measuring availability, the likely contamination of these measures by consumption patterns has received little notice (cf. Abbey, Scott, Oliansky, Quinn, & Andreski, 1990) and no research attention.

2. For the interested reader, a useful summary of current knowledge on the nature of drunk driving, and of much of the literature in this area, can be found in the *Surgeon General's Workshop on Drunk Driving: Background papers* (Department of Health and Human Services, 1989).

6

Methods for the Acquisition of Indicator Data

Previous chapters have discussed a number of major points that bear on the use of indicators to index community alcohol and other drug use and related problems. These include (1) the importance of collecting data at the level most proximate to the phenomena of interest (i.e., the community), (2) the fact that community indicators represent functional parts of community systems and thus reflect the ongoing needs of those systems rather than the needs of researchers, and (3) the resulting need for complementary surveys in the analysis of community alcohol and other drug use and related problems. In this chapter, the implications of these issues for the collection of indicator data are discussed and we turn our attention to the actual process of indicator data collection and analysis.

Communities are unlikely to collect and report data that meet all the needs of community researchers uniformly. Indeed, because indicator data are designed to meet the needs of the community systems that generate them, the researcher needs to search creatively (and often doggedly) for data sufficiently precise to allow quantitative analysis.

The need for precision in the acquisition and use of community indicator data dictates an iterative, multistep process. The steps of this process include (1) determination of the appropriate level of geographic and temporal aggregation for the study at hand, (2) definition of indicators between and within communities under consideration, (3) establishment of rigorous data search procedures, and (4) stable data management procedures for processing heterogeneous community data. Steps 1 through 3 iterate until either well-defined indicators at the appropriate geographic and temporal levels of aggregation are obtained or the search is abandoned.

LEVELS OF GEOGRAPHIC AND TEMPORAL AGGREGATION

Within any study, the requirements of temporal specificity are often relatively easy to determine. If the study design is cross-sectional, the goal is to obtain data for a specific time period. For example, data from the U.S. Census may be extremely useful if the time period under consideration matches the census timetable (e.g., 1990) but of limited use if not (e.g., 1995). One-time surveys, such as a school survey of drug use, are relevant if they are conducted at the time of the study but less so if they are out of date. Judgment must be exercised as to the temporal stability of out-of-date cross-sectional data, but in general, the poorer the correspondence between the study period and the date of data collection, the less likely the data are to be useful. In contrast, for time-series studies, data that are collected periodically are necessary, and frequently collected data (e.g., monthly as opposed to annual) are desired because they provide a greater number of data points for analysis. Some types of data (e.g., death certificate data) provide a high level of temporal specificity, whereas others are much less precise (e.g., the number of full-time law enforcement officers, a measure of local enforcement capacity, at the state level is measured as of October 31 of each year).

Determining the correct geographical strata for the data collection process can be a more complex process. The first step is to define the community of interest. If the community as defined for a research project bears no relation to the definitions used by the community systems that collect indicator data, data that fit the defined community will be impossible to obtain. Under ideal research conditions, the investigator will exercise some control over the community definition process. In this case, community definitions may be based on both substantive (e.g., whether the community shares a common culture) and methodological (e.g., whether the community is large enough to provide sufficient numbers of cases) grounds. In the real world, this ideal is seldom reached. Funding agencies, program directors, or local community interest groups usually make decisions about community boundaries. Thus, it is necessary for researchers to employ procedures for defining communities precisely in geographic terms within the boundaries already established by someone else and to locate data sources that can map onto these boundaries.

Table 6.1 summarizes the advantages and disadvantages of collecting data at various levels of geographic aggregation. Three of the more common levels of aggregation (county, city, and neighborhood) are shown as examples.[1] The data characteristics illustrated in the table are (1) uniformity, (2) cost, (3) sensitivity to local variation, and (4) availability.

Uniformity refers to the extent to which data tend to be similar across communities—a key characteristic when comparing communities but irrelevant to a study of a single community. Uniformity is generally

Table 6.1

Advantages and Disadvantages of Three Levels
of Aggregation of Indicator Data

Data Characteristics	Level of Data Aggregation		
	County	City	Neighborhood
Uniformity	High	Medium	Low
Cost	Low	Medium	High
Sensitivity	Low	Medium	High
Availability	High	Medium	Low

higher at higher levels of aggregation because regulations or standardized procedures for data collection and recording are more likely to exist at these levels.

The *cost* of obtaining archival data usually increases at lower levels of aggregation, primarily because such data are less likely to be maintained in electronic form and there is less often a budget or staff dedicated to providing such data to outside persons. It may also be the case that, although data can be aggregated to represent a small geographic area (e.g., police data at the precinct or beat level), they are not so aggregated by the agency or system that generates them. Thus, obtaining data at low levels of aggregation is more likely to require expenditures by the agency or the researcher.

Sensitivity to local variation denotes the extent to which data at one level of aggregation (e.g., counties) provide data relevant or useful in indexing variables in the smaller jurisdictions it includes (e.g., towns, cities, and rural areas). Sensitivity will naturally be higher at lower levels of aggregation.

Availability refers to the relative ease in acquiring data. As a general rule, county-level indicator data exist for a number of different areas of interest, but few indicators are available at the neighborhood level. Particularly when periodically collected data are desired, the lower the level of aggregation, the less likely it is that indicator data will exist.

Even if indicator data exist, they may be difficult to retrieve (e.g., paper-and-pencil intake and tracking records of a local detox program). Data may exist but be unobtainable. For example, the profit margins and plans for expansion or contraction of local businesses might serve as indicators of the health of the local economy. Such data are unlikely to be available to planners or evaluators, however.

In summary, each possible level of aggregation involves unique problems and opportunities for the researcher. The higher levels of aggregation (e.g., counties, cities) typically offer higher availability of data, higher uniformity of data, and low cost. But low sensitivity to local variation may be a serious drawback. At the lowest levels of aggregation, costs tend to be higher, whereas availability and uniformity are lower. Nevertheless, the high level of sensitivity to local variations offered by such data is a valuable asset and may override other considerations. An intermediate level of aggregation (represented by city-level data in Table 6.1) offers data of moderate cost, uniformity, availability, and sensitivity. In general, the process of collecting data at various levels of geographic aggregation involves trade-offs between data uniformity, cost, and availability on the one hand and sensitivity to local conditions on the other.

Table 6.1 provides some basic guidelines. The specific research project, however, will determine their application in selecting an appropriate level of aggregation. Examples of factors that affect the choice of level of aggregation include the following:

1. The nature of the particular community. There is a tremendous amount of variation among cities, counties, and other geopolitical units. The relative merits of city- and county-level data portrayed in Table 6.1 apply when a city or community is one of many in a county. However, many cities are, for all intents and purposes, identical to the county in which they are located (e.g., the city may account for 90% of the population and 85% of the land area of the county).

2. The level of aggregation at which data are available. Within the context of a given study, the optimal level of aggregation of one indicator (e.g., crime) may not be optimal for another (e.g., health). For example, if useful crime data are readily available at the level of the police district or beat, but health data can be obtained only for the city as a whole, it may be necessary to aggregate the crime data to the city level to provide comparable data across indicators.

On the other hand, a community may have poorly defined boundaries, as is sometimes true of neighborhoods. In such cases, different definitions of the neighborhood's boundaries may be established to accommodate different indicators (e.g., police district for crime indicators, census tracts or zip codes for demographic measures, the local school district for educational data, and one or more voting precincts for information on political participation). Here, the fuzziness of community boundaries works in the researcher's favor, although it will still be important to justify the levels of aggregation employed.

3. The design and goals of the study. The design of a particular study also affects which data characteristics take precedence. For example, the study might concern an intervention designed to reduce the number of drug overdoses in a large city. Only a limited number of indicators (e.g., emergency room admissions for drug overdose or deaths due to drug overdose) would be valid measures of the intended outcome. Availability of such indicators would be a crucial factor, whereas cost would be considered less important (assuming the study itself has important implications). For a large city, sensitivity to local variation would not be a key factor, and because only one community is involved, uniformity across communities would have little relevance.

On the other hand, evaluation of two different types of interventions, each aimed at reducing alcohol use and related problems in a small rural community, would require high uniformity (because two communities are to be compared) and high sensitivity to local variation because the target areas are small. Availability of any particular indicator would be less important because the objectives of the intervention are broadly defined. Here, cost could be balanced against availability. One might choose (1) indicators with low availability and low cost (e.g., electronic injury data from local trauma centers, available at no charge but with a lengthy procedure for approval of the release of confidential information and no guarantee that approval would be granted), and/or (2) indicators with high availability and high cost (e.g., a magnetic tape from a state injury database, requiring several hours of expensive programming time but easily ordered over the telephone).

AREAL MAPPING

Researchers using indicators are often faced with less than ideal geographic and temporal units of aggregation. Often, a given research project will require indicators for areas that are not easily defined by existing geopolitical boundaries. In these cases, the need for data covering a precise geographic area must be balanced against the available resources. For example, it may be possible to review written arrest records and select only those within a specific neighborhood. But if this is not feasible given the time or budget limitations of the research, data for a set of police districts that corresponds fairly closely to the neighborhood may be acceptable.

A certain degree of flexibility must also be maintained because different types of data are collected for different geopolitical units, and geopolitical units change over time. If a city is chosen as the preferred level of aggregation, some data will be obtainable only for the county, school district, congressional district, or some other area. After every possible source for similar data for the exact area of the community has been exhausted, data for a different geopolitical unit at a different level of aggregation may be the only alternative.

Maps

It is crucial to obtain maps before beginning to collect indicator data. Maps are essential in determining specific geographic boundaries for data at various levels of aggregation, and maps of each type of division for which data are collected are essential tools. Needed maps may include school districts and school attendance zones, voting precincts, police districts, aldermanic districts, zip codes, and census tracts.

Maps allow investigators to match the areas in which indicators are available to the area(s) of research interest. This step is important because indicator data may be available specifically for the area of interest, and it may be more or less expensive or time-consuming to obtain data for that area alone. For example, if a Registrar of Voters office must program its computer for a special run to produce data broken down by voting precinct, it may be better to request data for the few precincts that make up the area(s) of interest rather than for the entire area for which data are available. Resources will be conserved if the investigator knows exactly which voting precincts are of interest before calling the registrar to request data.

It is not at all unusual for zip code boundaries to change, especially if data are collected for more than a few years. More rarely, census tract, city, or other boundaries change over time. These changes can be tracked to maintain the precise geographic definition of the area(s) of interest. Because boundaries change over time, it is important to get up-to-date maps (not always a straightforward task).

If the only maps available are out of date, it is sometimes possible to procure information about how boundaries have changed since the map was made. It is often also worthwhile to check more than one source. For example, the Chamber of Commerce may have a 10-year-old map of local school districts, whereas the County Board of Education may have a more recent version. In the search for maps, the researcher should not confine himself or herself to conventional or obvious sources. The resourceful investigator will seek maps from planning commissions, automobile clubs, or anywhere else maps may be found. Maps are also available on CD-ROM. For example, detailed zip code maps are often difficult to locate, but may be purchased on CD-ROM. Street maps on CD-ROM can be used in mapping point data (e.g., data from the Fatal Accident Reporting System, in which crashes are located by the nearest street intersection) so that these data can be converted to other spatial units such as zip codes, census tracts, or police districts.

As an alternative to the use of traditional maps, Graphic Information Systems (GISs) may be used to track geographic data. These systems, which integrate graphics with a relational database for the purpose of managing data about graphic locations (Ripple, 1989), are particularly useful where data are extremely fine grained (e.g., cross streets). GISs (e.g., Mapinfo) are currently available for PC users and allow the user to create layered maps displaying data collected at various units of aggregation. These maps provide the user with the capability of placing within a geographically defined area events such as car crashes and environmental features of interest (e.g., alcohol outlets, streets, cross streets closest to survey respondent home locations). Of particular use are typologically integrated, geographically encoded reference (TIGER) files. These files, available from the census bureau, present street-level maps for the entire United States and contain street addresses for most urbanized and incorporated areas. Although TIGER files occupy large amounts of disk space, they provide an invaluable tool in the analysis of spatially distributed data. Furthermore, they can be used with most mapping software packages. At an elementary level, TIGER files provide the technology for the generation of maps that are understandable to users of the data. In their advanced applications, TIGER files allow the researcher to develop coordinated systems for use in the analysis of spatially distributed data.

Determining which geographic units (e.g., which police districts, census tracts, or zip codes) are included in the area(s) of interest is usually a simple matter if the area is a county or city, but can be quite time-consuming. This is particularly true because some units, notably school districts and census tracts, use boundaries difficult to locate on street maps (e.g., natural features such as small streams, units of latitude and longitude, or a line drawn between two points). When written descriptions of borders exist, they can be very useful and should be obtained, if possible. Follow-up telephone calls may be required, however, as when the name of a highway is used in the border description but maps show only the numbers of the local highways, or when a new subdivision shown on one street map does not appear on another map. Here, investigators may want to use GISs if telephone follow-up proves inefficient.

Zip Codes

It is particularly important to identify the zip codes corresponding to the area(s) of interest. This is the most practical means for combining indicator data with survey data. Most survey respondents know their zip codes, but few are able to identify other geographic units locating their places of residence (e.g., census tract, voting precinct, or police district). The use of zip codes thus enables the researcher to focus a survey on an area of interest that is part of a larger jurisdiction. For random-digit dialing surveys, telephone exchanges (which approximately match zip code areas in some jurisdictions) can be obtained. A caveat must be issued, however. Telephone company practices vary considerably by geographic area and change within geographic areas over time. In general, the trend has been away from grouping temporally contiguous telephones within common exchanges and area codes. As a result, geographically adjacent residents may have different exchanges.

FINAL COMMENT ON AGGREGATION

It is worth evaluating the degree to which available data differ from the desired level of aggregation before abandoning state or national sources of data. Some sense of the degree to which data levels differ can be achieved through comparisons of population sizes. At 10-year intervals, population figures down to the census block can be obtained from the U.S. Bureau of the Census. These can be aggregated to represent the available versus the ideal level of aggregation. For instance, a large city may represent 90% of the population of the entire county. Here, county-level data may closely match city-level data, and county-level data available from a national data source might be substituted for city-level data. In another example, a school district might include a medium-sized city plus several nearby small towns. If 80% of the district enrollment consists of students from the city, it might be possible to use district-level data on dropout rates, obtained from the state education department.

ADDITIONAL TECHNICAL ISSUES
IN THE USE OF INDICATORS

Defining Indicators Within and Between Communities

For indicators to be useful (and not misleading) in community research, safeguards must be built into the data acquisition process to protect its integrity over the life of the collection period. Perhaps the most important of these safeguards involves indicator definition. An indicator may be defined along two dimensions: (1) what it means both to the system that generates it and to the researcher (i.e., what it will be used to represent), and (2) how it is generated.

A precise definition of the meaning of an indicator is critical because a term such as *narcotics arrests* may be used differently in different communities. Failure to reconcile these differences may introduce bias, error, or both into the measurement design. Moreover, certain indicators (e.g., arrests) are often used in research as surrogates for unmeasurable variables (e.g., crime). In such cases, investigators must clearly understand and articulate the conceptual and empirical relationships between the indicator and the variables of interest for meaningful analyses to be conducted.

Because pragmatic concerns often predominate in the process by which community systems generate indicator data, the careful examination of this process is critical to data interpretation. This point is well illustrated with the case of arrests for public drunkenness. In many areas (e.g., the state of New Hampshire), public drunkenness per se is not proscribed. Rather, problems involving inebriates are handled through other public order mechanisms, such as arrests for disorderly behavior. Furthermore, such arrests may be used less as a way of dealing with alcohol use than a way of clearing the streets of people likely to distract police officers going about their other law enforcement activities. Police in a high-crime area may arrest an inebriate either as a form of protective custody or as a way of quickly dispatching the problem. Here, rates of arrests for charges other than public drunkenness (e.g., disorderly conduct) may reflect rates of public intoxication, but the investigator must thoroughly understand police practices in dealing with inebriates to use and analyze these rates.

Published definitions exist for some indicators, especially those reported to national agencies such as the National Center for Health Statistics or the FBI. It is always wise to confirm these with local sources, because they may not be followed exactly by each local agency. Such definitions frequently change over time. For instance, due to a change in the penal code in 1981, some homicide statistics in California for 1981-1985 include assault with intent to commit murder.

Establishing Data Search Procedures

Central to the process of obtaining archival indicator data is the development of a structured procedure for locating and obtaining data. Particularly when dealing with more than one community, time periods spanning several years, or low levels of aggregation, search procedures can become sufficiently complex to require a significant amount of resources. Key components of an effective data search procedure are (1) a systematic method of identifying contact persons who can provide relevant data, (2) adequate record keeping, (3) continuous tracking and evaluation of the data requested and received, and (4) an electronic database for data archiving.

One of the principles to guide data search procedures is that data are more difficult, if not impossible, to disaggregate than to aggregate. Thus, data should be obtained at as low a level of aggregation as possible.

The other principle is that data should be obtained in the most efficient manner consistent with the required level of temporal and spatial specificity. This is accomplished by acquiring data from national or state sources whenever possible. In many cases, however, such sources are inadequate, because many national and state data sources are unable to provide information with the necessary degree of geographic or temporal specificity.

A Sample Data Management Procedure

Figure 6.1 is a simplified model of one data acquisition procedure. Each box within this system involves a series of steps that must be customized to the specific needs of the investigator.

Select Agency/Source to be Contacted. As can be seen in Figure 6.1, the first step in the data acquisition process involves selection of the agency, organization, or source to be contacted. As noted, the source may be a county database, a records department in a police department,

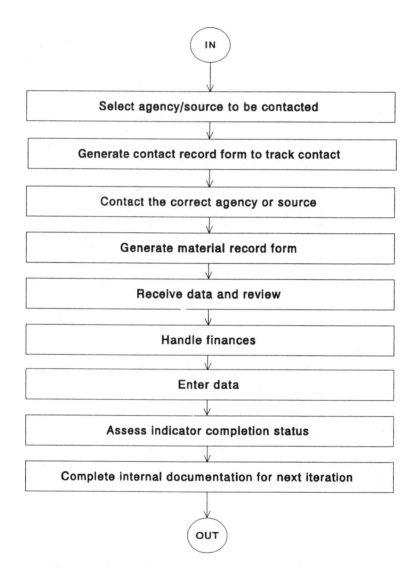

Figure 6.1. Data Acquisition Flow Chart

or some other entity. The identification of potential data sources should begin with national and state-level sources of data. Where national or state data exist in sufficient detail, they are much more likely than local-level data to be in electronic form. Moreover, a good national or state data source can provide data for a number of different communities at once, greatly reducing the time and effort required to obtain the data. Often, however, only summary data can be obtained from national and state sources. Where national and state sources fail to provide adequate data, the investigator must (1) contact potential community data sources, (2) ask for referrals if the initial contacts prove to be unproductive, (3) track leads until the location of the data in question is determined, and (4) establish a permanent archive of sources to be contacted for future similar data. The establishment of systems for tracking contacts not only provides for data continuity within communities but also reduces duplication of effort and results in savings of resources.

The compilation of a bank of community data sources is accomplished through a series of contacts, based on known contact persons if possible, but failing this, based on a series of cold calls. Potential contacts may be identified through telephone books, brainstorming, or past experience with the community or similar communities.

Generate Contact Record Form. Upon selection of the source most likely to provide relevant data, a contact record needs to be generated prior to initial contact. This step is indicated by the second box in Figure 6.1. Examples of the types of information that may be useful to include are: (1) the community name and indicator of interest; (2) the name, position, and phone number of the contact; and (3) a dated summary of conversations relating to data acquisition. The contact record may also contain relevant information on any letters that must be written prior to data release and other persons to contact. As an alternative, contact software currently available to run on a variety of platforms may be used.

There are several purposes of the contact record. First, it allows one to maintain a permanent record of the individuals contacted, allowing follow-up with individuals who fail to send materials promised. Second, the contact record provides a starting place for subsequent iterations of the data search process (e.g., collecting data the following year). This is particularly important for multiyear studies because memories and staff stability cannot be depended on over long periods of time. Third, by noting dead ends, the contact record eliminates nonproductive contact activity. Finally, the contact record documents the search process (necessary to meet reporting requirements and to write research reports) and establishes guidelines in conducting follow-up research.

Contact the Correct Agency or Source. The third step is making the actual contact. Contacts made by telephone allow one to identify a series of referral persons expeditiously if the initial contact person does not have the desired data. Follow-up letters are required (1) when an organization requires a written request for data, (2) to aid in establishing the legitimacy of the study, or (3) to explain further the nature of the request when the desired data are complex or difficult to describe briefly. Some indicator data are used internally and are not generally requested by members of the public. An example is information on the percentages of persons participating in outpatient drug counseling programs who abuse a particular type of drug. Here, data may be more difficult to acquire because no procedures for releasing them may exist. It is helpful to know enough about the contacted source to determine whether the requested data are public, internal, or proprietary. In some cases, a database containing confidential information (e.g., names) can be stripped of that information and released.

Generate Material Record Form. The fourth step shown in Figure 6.1 is to generate a material record form. A material record form can be partially completed when the correct contact has been identified and the data have been requested. Much as the contact record tracks the flow of contacts in data acquisition, the material record form tracks the flow of relevant materials. This form indicates (1) the source from which data were requested (for documentation and follow-up purposes), (2) the indicator or indicators represented, (3) the community or communities to which the data apply, (4) the time periods to which they pertain, and (5) when necessary, payment information. As with the contact record, these forms serve not only to document the project but also to save time in subsequent data collection periods. When the data have been received, a brief description of the data may be added to the material record form.

Receive and Review Data. Data not only must be tracked, they must also be reviewed. This step is critical because data provided sometimes do not correspond to data promised.

Finances. The sixth step involves handling payment for data and reconciling the payments with existing project budgets. This step may seem trivial, but failure to reimburse data sources promptly may strain important relationships that must be maintained throughout the lifetime of the research.

Enter Data and Assess Indicator Completion Status. Following data entry, the data on hand are assessed to determine whether or not a given indicator has been completed. The iterative nature of this procedure cannot be overstated. If complete data for the indicator in question have not been obtained, it is necessary to return to the first step and select either an original or an alternative source of data.

Complete Internal Documentation. Finally, data documentation is completed. Documentation includes a review of the contact and material record forms. The purpose of this step is to ensure that the source and contents of the data have been adequately recorded, both to guide the continuing acquisition of data and to serve as a resource for future data collection efforts.

Costs

Investigators using data acquisition procedures of the sort presented here inevitably must address issues of cost. First, the research design may require the use of proprietary data systems typically compiled by for-profit organizations. For example, the county-level economic and demographic data available annually from NPA Inc. are relevant indicators for some studies.

Furthermore, acquisition of even readily available data will involve costs for mailing, photocopying, staff, or computer time. Such costs may be considerable. One study required that the California Department of Justice write a subroutine to compile monthly arrest data for several towns over a 10-year period. As state and local budgets continue to decline, it will become increasingly likely that agencies will request payment for assisting researchers in the compilation and retrieval of indicator data.

Finely grained data may be available from some sources, but at prohibitive cost. For example, monthly arrests by ethnic group by crime may be obtainable, but the cost may not be justifiable for a given research objective. Less expensive yearly arrest figures may suffice and be readily available. Investigators must make a trade-off between scientific sophistication and budgetary concerns, or, in the case of studies using multiple indicators, a number of trade-offs.

Data Management Issues

Management of the indicator data collection process requires a systematic approach. Often a contact must be pursued intensively through a series of telephone calls and letters. These must be carefully tracked and decisions made as to when a change in tactics is appropriate or a contact should be designated as unproductive. Experience suggests that a contact who initially appears to be ideal may never provide usable data, however, whereas an initially unproductive contact may prove to be a good data source with sufficient persistence and clarity in communicating data needs.

Data management can be a complex process. This complexity arises, in part, because of the degree of variability in the data across time and geography. Often, similar data are available for different geographic areas and time periods across communities. For example, a target community may have automated its arrest records in 1980, making it possible to break down arrests by police district. A comparison community may not have automated records until 1989, however. On the other hand, the comparison community's data system may be more sophisticated, allowing retrieval of monthly arrest records, whereas the target community can provide only annual totals.

Where many communities are involved, the question arises of whether to catalog data by indicator or by community. One possible method is to combine the two cataloging methods—data are filed first by indicator, then within each indicator by community.

Finally, it is sometimes necessary to enter and catalog data that are later superseded by more adequate data. Careful data management is required to ensure that old data are stored or deleted so that the more adequate data are actually used in analysis.

Data Archiving

Once indicator data are in hand, they must be archived in electronic form. Typically, archiving involves the development of a database or series of databases that allow for the entry of data by indicator area (e.g., health, crime). Also needed are markers for (1) the community from which the data were collected, (2) the source, (3) the unit of aggregation (e.g., city, county), and (4) the time period to which the data pertain.

Clear documentation must be kept noting database oddities and non-uniformities. For example, if data on narcotics arrests include marijuana arrests for some years and not others, this fact must be noted so that analyses do not produce spurious results.

SUMMARY

This chapter provides a technical "how to do it" approach to both the collection and the management of community indicator data. It began by discussing the issue of geographic and temporal aggregation. This is a major issue because the selection of inappropriate aggregation or the simultaneous use of data sources mismatched in terms of aggregation poses one of the greatest threats to the internal validity of community studies. Additionally, we considered the use of areal mapping as a technical means for addressing the problem of aggregation. We concluded by presenting a system for monitoring the data acquisition process. Specifically, this system illustrates the iterative process by which contacts are made for data collection, contacts are followed up, data are tracked and entered, and finances are handled.

NOTE

1. Other levels of aggregation commonly used are (in approximate order of decreasing size of the geographic area covered) nation, state, sheriff's department jurisdiction, metropolitan statistical area, area code, school district, voting precinct, police district, zip code, census tract or (in rural areas) block numbering area, census block, cross-street, and exact street address.

7

Comment

This monograph began with a call for the collection and analysis of community indicator data addressing substance abuse. It then presented the argument for a systems perspective approach to the collection of such data. As indicated above, the theory of communities underlying the systems perspective has implications for data collection and analysis, perhaps the most important of which is that data have to be viewed as a product of the community systems generating them. We presented material on relevant community indicators and the use of general population survey data as a complement to indicator data. We concluded with a presentation of the technical process appropriate to the collection and analysis of indicator data.

We have attempted to present both the strengths and the weakness of community indicator data in substance abuse research. Clearly, the strengths are numerous. First, community indicators data provide a much finer resolution than is provided by existing state or national measures. Given both the need to address substance-use-related issues within a local context and the great variability of substance-related use patterns and problems, this is a critical issue. Second, community indicators data are sometimes readily available and significantly cheaper than primary data collection (e.g., through surveys). This latter consideration, given the current availability of research funding, is a nontrivial matter. Third, community indicators data cover a range of mediating and outcome variables related to substance abuse and substance-related problems. From a systems perspective, this is a major advantage. Fourth, community indicators data may be available over long periods of time, allowing the application of sophisticated time series analyses.

A number of potential weaknesses of indicators data must also be acknowledged, however. First, community indicators data may not be available in usable form in many communities or may not meet the temporal and spatial requirements of the research. Indeed, the gap between the complexities required by research designs and available data often comes as a surprise to new researchers attempting to do indicator-based research. Second, these data may be expensive and labor intensive to obtain. Here we note the difference between data that are "readily available" and those that are "without cost." Third, community indicators data may be grossly misleading without an understanding of the community systems that produce them. Again, these data may not be taken at face value from a systems perspective.

One issue that remains to be considered involves whether it is possible to establish an exhaustive list of community substance abuse indicators. Although such an endeavor might appear tempting, from the viewpoint of a systems theory of indicators, it is inadvisable. Because community needs differ and indicators are themselves the products of communities meeting those needs, we expect community indicators to differ by community. Alcohol price is likely to bear a different relationship to consumption in a community where brand substitution is common than one where it is not. To take another illustration, the rates of certain crimes are more likely to be influenced by illegal drug consumption in communities where those crimes are linked to illegal drug consumption. Again, we focus on the need to develop synthetic or theoretically driven models of drug use prior to the establishment of a list of substance abuse indicators. In sum, the indicators discussed in Chapter 4 should be seen as illustrative, not exhaustive.

We end this chapter by noting that indicators are not a panacea to communities or researchers who may believe that they provide a tool for cheap, easy community research. On the other hand, in the hands of competent, thoughtful and careful researchers, indicators can be a powerful tool for community research. When combined with other forms of complementary data collection, indicators provide one vehicle for developing an understanding of the complex and dynamic systems that underlie community substance abuse and related problems.

References

Abbey, A., Scott, R. O., Oliansky, D. M., Quinn, B., & Andreski, P. M. (1990). Subjective, social and physical availability. I. Their interrelationships. *International Journal of the Addictions, 25,* 889-910.

Abbey, A., Scott, R. O., & Smith, M. J. (1993). Physical, subjective, and social availability: Their relationship to alcohol consumption in rural and urban areas. *Addiction, 88,* 489-499.

Adams, F. G., & Klein, L. R. (1991). Performance of quarterly econometric models of the United States: A new round of model comparisons. In L. R. Klein (Ed.), *Comparative performance of U.S. econometric models* (pp. 46-63). New York: Oxford University Press.

Adams, J. S. (1976). *A comparison atlas of America's great cities.* Minneapolis: University of Minnesota Press.

Aitken, S. S., & Zobeck, T. (1985). Trends in alcohol-related fatal motor-vehicle accidents for 1983. *Alcohol Health and Research World, 9*(4), 60-62.

American Chamber of Commerce Research Association. (1987). *Intercity cost of living index.* Indianapolis, IN: Author.

Baker, S. P., O'Neill, B., Ginsburg, M. J., & Li, G. (1992). *The injury fact book* (2nd ed.). New York: Oxford University Press.

Beitel, G., Sharp, M., & Glauz, W. (1975). Probability of arrest while driving under the influence of alcohol. *Journal of Studies on Alcohol, 36,* 237-256.

Blose, J., & Holder, H. D. (1987). Liquor-by-the-drink and alcohol-related traffic crashes: A natural experiment using time-series analysis. *Journal of Studies on Alcohol, 48,* 52-60.

British Journal of Addiction. (1987). No "alcoholism" please, we're British. *British Journal of Addiction, 82,* 1059-1060.

Bureau of Justice Statistics. (1992). *Crime in the United States, 1991* (NCJ-139563). Washington, DC: Department of Justice.

California Hospital Discharge Data Program. (1993). *Profile of hospital patients.* Sacramento: Office of Statewide Health Planning and Development.

California Statewide Integrated Traffic Records System. (1993). Sacramento: Department of California Highway Patrol.

Carmines, E. G., & Zellner, R. (1979). *Reliability and validity assessment.* Beverly Hills: Sage.

Caulkins, J. P., & Padman, R. (1993). Quantity discounts and quality premia for illicit drugs. *Journal of the American Statistical Association, 88,* 548-575.

Chaiken, J. M., & Chaiken, M. R. (1990). Drugs and predatory crime. In M. Tonry & J. Q. Wilson (Eds.), *Drugs and crime* (pp. 203-239). Chicago: University of Chicago Press.

Chaloupka, F. J. (1993). Effects of price on alcohol-related problems. *Alcohol Health & Research World, 17*(1), 46-53.

Champagne, C. L., Crowe, M. J., Flaming, K. H., & Judd, E. P. (1976). *A manual for health related urban indicators.* Denver: Denver Urban Observatory, National League of Cities, Office of Policy Development and Analysis, Department of Housing and Urban Development.

Clark, W. B., & Hilton, M. E. (1991). *Alcohol in America: Drinking practices and problems.* Albany: State University of New York Press.

Coate, D., & Grossman, M. (1988). The effects of alcoholic beverage prices and legal drinking ages on youth alcohol use. *Journal of Law and Economics, 31*(1), 145-171.

Cook, P. J., & Moore, M. J. (1991, October). *Taxation of alcoholic beverages.* Paper presented at the NIAAA Workshop on Economic and Socioeconomic Issues in the Prevention of Alcohol-Related Problems, Bethesda, MD.

Cook, P. J., & Tauchen, G. (1982). The effect of liquor taxes on heavy drinking. *Bell Journal of Economics, 13,* 379-390.

Dawkins, R. (1982). *The extended phenotype.* Oxford, UK: Freeman.

Department of Health and Human Services. (1989). *Surgeon General's Workshop on Drunk Driving: Background papers.* Washington, DC: Government Printing Office.

Department of Health and Human Services, National Institute on Drug Abuse. (1991). *Annual Emergency Room Data, 1990* (Statistical Series I, Number 10-A). Washington, DC: Government Printing Office.

Department of Health and Human Services, Substance Abuse and Mental Health Services Administration, Office of Applied Statistics. (1992). *Highlights from 1991 National Drug and Alcoholism Treatment Unit Survey (NDATUS).* Bethesda, MD: Public Health Service.

Department of Justice, Federal Bureau of Investigation. (1992). *Crime in the United States.* Washington, DC: Government Printing Office.

Department of Treasury, U.S. Customs Service. (1991). *U.S. customs—update 1990.* Washington, DC: Author.

Diamond, J. (1992). Sweet death. *Natural History, 2*(3), 2-6.

Drug Enforcement Administration, U.S. Department of Justice. (1992). *1991 Domestic Cannabis Eradication/Suppression Program.* Washington, DC: Department of Justice.

Evans, L. (1990). The fraction of traffic fatalities attributable to alcohol. *Accident Analysis and Prevention, 22,* 587-602.

Executive Office of the President. (1992). *National drug control strategy: Budget summary.* Washington, DC: Office of National Drug Control Policy.

Federal Bureau of Investigation. (1992). *Crime in the United States 1991.* Washington, DC: Author.

Flax, M. J. (1978). *Survey of urban indicator data, 1970-1977.* Washington, DC: Urban Institute.

Greene, W. H. (1993). *Econometric analysis* (2nd ed.). New York: Macmillan.

Grossman, M. (1991, October). *The economic analysis of addictive behavior.* Paper presented at the NIAAA Conference Economic and Socioeconomic Issues in the Prevention of Alcohol-Related Problems, Bethesda, MD.

Grossman, M., Coate, D., and Arluck, G.M. (1987) Price sensitivity of alcoholic beverages in the United States. In H. D. Holder (ed.), *Control Issues in Alcohol Abuse Prevention: Strategies for Communities,* Greenwich, CT: JAI Press, pp. 169-198.

Gruenewald, P. J. (1991). Loss of control drinking among first offender drunk drivers. *Alcoholism: Clinical and Experimental Research, 15,* 634-639.

Gruenewald, P. J. (1994). Alcohol problems and the control of availability. In M. E Hilton & G. Bloss (Eds.), *Economics and the prevention of alcohol-related problems* (pp. 59-90; NIAAA Research Monograph #25). Bethesda, MD: Government Printing Office.

Gruenewald, P. J., Hill, M., Treno, A., & Taff, G. (1993, September). *Community indicators related to substance use: The complementarity of archival and survey data.* Paper presented at the conference Community Score Cards: Measures of Success or Failure in Fighting Substance Abuse, Boston.

Gruenewald, P. J., Madden, P., & Janes, K. (1992). Alcohol availability and the formal power and resources of state alcohol beverage control agencies. *Alcoholism: Clinical and Experimental Research, 16,* 591-597.

Gruenewald, P. J., Millar, A. B., & Treno, A. J. (1993). Alcohol availability and the ecology of drinking behavior. *Alcohol Health & Research World, 17*(1), 39-45.

Gruenewald, P. J., Millar, A. B., Treno, A. J., Yang, Z., Ponicki, W. R., & Roeper, P. The geography of availability and drinking and driving. *Addiction, 91*(7), 967-983.

Gruenewald, P. J., & Nephew, T. (1991, June). *Consumption and death: The dynamics of alcohol consumption patterns.* Paper presented at the Annual Meeting of the Research Society on Alcoholism, Marco Island, FL.

Gruenewald, P. J., & Nephew, T. (1994). Drinking in California: Theoretical and empirical analyses of alcohol consumption patterns. *Addiction, 89,* 707-723.

Gruenewald, P. J., & Ponicki, W. R. (1995a). The relationship of outlet densities and alcohol sales to cirrhosis mortality. *Journal of Studies on Alcohol, 56,* 635-641.

Gruenewald, P. J., & Ponicki, W. R. (1995b). The relationship of the retail availability of alcohol and alcohol sales to alcohol related traffic crashes. *Accident Analysis and Prevention, 27*(2), 249-259.

Gruenewald, P. J., Ponicki, W. R., & Holder, H. D. (1993). The relationship of outlet densities to alcohol consumption: A time series cross-sectional analysis. *Alcoholism: Clinical and Experimental Research, 17*(1), 38-47.

Hallan, J. B., & Holder, H. D. (1986a). Analysis of insurance benefit plans for alcoholism treatment through computer simulations. Parts I and II. *Computers in Psychiatry/Psychology, 8*(1), 12-15.

Hallan, J. B., & Holder, H. D. (1986b). Analysis of insurance benefit plans for alcoholism treatment through computer simulations. Parts I and II. *Computers in Psychiatry/Psychology, 8*(2), 112-15.

Hause, J., Voas, R., & Chavez, E. (1982). Conducting voluntary roadside surveys: The Stockton experience. In M. R. Valverius (Ed.), *Proceedings of the Satellite Conference to the Eighth International Conference on Alcohol, Drugs and Traffic Safety* (pp. 104-113). Stockholm: Swedish Council for Information on Alcohol and Other Drugs.

Holder, H. D. (1974). *Alternative approaches to the public inebriate problem in metropolitan areas: A summary of findings for Atlanta, Georgia and Baltimore, Maryland.* Raleigh, NC: Human Ecology Institute.

Holder, H. D. (1992). What is a community and what are implications for prevention trials for reducing alcohol problems? In H. D. Holder & J. M. Howard (Eds.), *Community prevention trials for alcohol problems: Methodological issues* (pp. 16-33). Westport, CT: Praeger.

Holder, H. D., & Blose, J. O. (1983). Prevention of alcohol-related traffic problems: Computer simulation of alternative strategies. *Journal of Safety Research, 14*(3), 115-129.

Holder, H. D., & Blose, J. O. (1987). Reduction of community alcohol problems: Computer simulation experiments in three counties. *Journal of Studies on Alcohol, 48,* 124-135.

Holder, H. D., & Blose, J. O. (1991). Typical patterns and cost of alcoholism treatment across a variety of populations and providers. *Alcoholism: Clinical and Experimental Research, 15*(2), 190-195.

Holder, H. D., Grube, J. W., Gruenewald, P. J., Saltz, R. F., Treno, A. J., & Voas, R. (1995). Community approaches to prevention of alcohol-involved accidents. *Drug and alcohol abuse reviews* (Vol. 7, pp. 175-194). Totowa, NJ: Humana.

Holder, H. D., Lennox, R. D., & Blose, J. O. (1992). *The economic benefits of alcoholism treatment: A summary of twenty years of research.* Berkeley, CA: Prevention Research Center.

Holder, H. D., Miner, W., & Kible, B. (1993a). *SIMCOM: Simulated Community Model of Alcohol Use and Abuse. Causal Model of Community Alcohol Use and Abuse, Section I: Overview of Model Rationale and Design.* Chapel Hill, NC: Prevention Research Center.

Holder, H. D., Miner, W., & Kible, B. (1993b). *SIMCOM: Simulated Community Model of Alcohol Use and Abuse. Drinking and Driving Subsystem, Section I: Description of Subsystem Model.* Chapel Hill, NC: Prevention Research Center.

Holder, H. D., Miner, W., & Kible, B. (1993c). *SIMCOM: Simulated Community Model of Alcohol Use and Abuse. Consumption Subsystem, Section I: Description of Subsystem Model.* Chapel Hill, NC: Prevention Research Center.

Holder, H. D., & Parker, R. N. (1992). Effect of alcoholism treatment on cirrhosis mortality: A 20-year multivariate time series analysis. *British Journal of Addiction, 87,* 1263-1274.

Holder, H. D., & Wallack, L. (1986). Contemporary perspectives for preventing alcohol problems: An empirically-derived model. *Journal of Public Health Policy, 7,* 324-339.

Hughes, A. L. (1992). The prevalence of illicit drug use in six metropolitan areas in the United States: Results from the 1991 National Household Survey on Drug Abuse. *British Journal of Addiction, 87,* 1481-1485.

Hughes, J. W. (1973). *Urban indicators, metropolitan evolution and public policy.* New Brunswick, NJ: Rutgers University, Center for Urban Policy Research.

Hunt, D. (1990). Drugs and consensual crimes: Drug dealing and prostitution. In M. Tonry & J. Q. Wilson (Eds.), *Drugs and crime* (pp. 159-202). Chicago: University of Chicago Press.

Innes, J. E. (1990). *Knowledge and public policy: The search for meaningful indicators (2nd ed.).* New Brunswick: Transaction.

Janes, K., & Gruenewald, P. J. (1991). The role of formal law in alcohol control systems: A comparison among states. *American Journal of Drug and Alcohol Abuse, 17* (2), 199-214.

Johnson, B. D., Williams, T., Dei, K. A., & Sanabria, H. (1990). Drug abuse in the inner city: Impact on hard-drug users and the community. In M. Tonry & J. Q. Wilson (Eds.), *Drugs and crime* (pp. 9-67). Chicago: University of Chicago Press.

Johnston, L. D., O'Malley, P. M., & Bachman, J. G. (1992). *Smoking, drinking, and illicit drug use among American secondary school students, college students, and young adults.* Washington, DC: Government Printing Office.

Johnston, L. D., O'Malley, P. M., & Bachman, J. G. (1993). *National study results on drug use from the Monitoring the Future study, 1975-1992* (Vol. 2). Rockville, MD: Department of Health and Human Services, National Institute on Drug Abuse.

Johnston, L. D., O'Malley, P. M., & Bachman, J. G. (1994). *National study results on drug use from the Monitoring the Future study, 1975-1993* (Vol. 1). Rockville, MD: Department of Health and Human Services, National Institute on Drug Abuse.

Join Together, Boston University School of Public Health, and Institute for Health Policy Heller School, Brandeis University. (1995). *How do we know that we are making a difference? A community substance abuse indicators handbook.* Boston: Authors.

Judge, G. G., Griffiths, W. E., Hill, R. C., Lutkepohl, H., & Lee, T-C. (1985). *The theory and practice of econometrics* (2nd ed.). New York: John Wiley.

Katzper, M., Ryback, R., & Hertzman, M. (1976). *Preliminary aspects of modeling and simulation for understanding alcohol utilization and the effects of regulatory policies.* Washington, DC: National Institute on Alcohol Abuse and Alcoholism.

Kenny, D. A. (1979). *Correlation and causality.* New York: John Wiley.

Kleiman, M. A. R., & Smith, K. D. (1990). State and local drug enforcement: In search of a strategy. In M. Tonry & J. Q. Wilson (Eds.), *Drugs and crime* (pp. 69-108). Chicago: University of Chicago Press.

Klein, L. R. (1991). *Comparative performance of U.S. econometric models.* New York: Oxford University Press.

Klitzner, M. D. (1994). Application of a systems approach to DWI. *Alcohol, Drugs, and Driving, 10*(3-4), 217-266.

Land, K. C., & Spilerman, S. (1975). *Social indicator models.* New York: Sage.

Leung, S. F., & Phelps, C. E. (1991, October). *"My kingdom for a drink. . .?" A review of estimates of the price sensitivity of demand for alcoholic beverages.* Paper presented at the NIAAA Workshop on Economic and Socioeconomic Issues in the Prevention of Alcohol-Related Problems, Bethesda, MD.

Levin, G., Roberts, E., & Hirsch, G. B. (1975). *The persistent poppy: A computer-aided search for heroin policy.* Cambridge, MA: Ballinger.

Levine, H. G. (1978). The discovery of addiction: Changing conceptions of habitual drunkenness in America. *Journal of Studies on Alcohol, 39,* 143-174.

MacRae, D., Jr. (1985). *Policy indicators: Links between social science and public debate.* Chapel Hill: University of North Carolina Press.

Maltz, M. D. (1984). *Recidivism.* New York: Academic.

Maquire, K., & Flanagan, T. J. (1991). *Sourcebook of criminal justice statistics—1990.* Washington, DC: Government Printing Office.

McFarland, D. D. (1975). Models involving social indicators of population and the quality of life. In K.C. Land & S. Spilerman (Eds.), *Social indicator models* (pp. 186-203). New York: Sage.

Meyers, A. R., Heeren, T., & Hingson, R. (1989). Cops and drivers: Police discretion and the enforcement of Maine's 1981 DUI law. *Journal of Criminal Justice, 15,* 361-368.

Model, K. E. (1993). The effect of marijuana decriminalization on hospital emergency room drug episodes: 1975-1978. *Journal of the American Statistical Association, 88,* 737-747.

Moore, M. H. (1990). Supply reduction and drug law enforcement. In M. Tonry & J. Q. Wilson (Eds.), *Drugs and crime* (pp. 109-157). Chicago: University of Chicago Press.

Moore, M. J., & Cook, P. J. (1991, October). *Taxation of alcoholic beverages.* Paper presented at the NIAAA Workshop on Economic and Socioeconomic Issues in the Prevention of Alcohol-Related Problems, Bethesda, MD.

Moskowitz, J. M. (1989). The primary prevention of alcohol problems: A critical review of the research literature. *Journal of Studies on Alcohol, 50,* 54-88.

Mounce, N., Pendleton, O., & Gonzales, O. (1988). *Alcohol involvement in Texas driver fatalities.* College Station: Texas A&M University, Texas Transportation Institute.

National Center for Health Statistics. (1992). *Catalog of Publications, 1990-91.* Atlanta, GA: Centers for Disease Control and Prevention.

National Center for Injury Prevention and Control. (1993). *The prevention of youth violence: A framework for community action.* Atlanta, GA: Centers for Disease Control and Prevention.

National Highway Traffic Safety Administration. (1992). *1991 alcohol fatal crash facts.* Washington, DC: Government Printing Office.

National Institute on Drug Abuse. (1989). *Overview of selected drug trends.* Washington, DC: Author.

National Institute on Drug Abuse. (1991). *National household survey on drug abuse: Main findings 1990.* Washington, DC: Government Printing Office.

National Institute of Justice. (1992). *1991 drug use forecasting annual report.* Washington, DC: Department of Justice.

Nelson, J. P. (1988). *Effects of regulation on alcoholic beverage consumption: Regression diagnostics and influential data.* University Park: Pennsylvania State University, Department of Economics.

Office of National Drug Control Policy. (1991). *National drug control strategy.* Washington, DC: Government Printing Office.

Parker, R. N. (1993). Alcohol and theories of homicide. In F. Adler & W. S. Laufer (Eds.), *New directions in criminological theory* (pp. 113-141). New Brunswick, CT: Transaction.

Perrine, M. W., Peck, R. C., & Fell, J. C. (1989). Epidemiologic perspectives on drunk driving. In *Surgeon General's Workshop on Drunk Driving: Background papers* (pp. 35-76). Bethesda, MD: Department of Health and Human Services.

Preble, E., & Casey, J. J., Jr. (1969). Taking care of business—the heroin user's life on the street. *International Journal of the Addictions, 4,* 1-24.

President's Commission on Organized Crime. (1986). *The impact: Organized crime today.* Washington, DC: Government Printing Office.

Puckett, C. D. (1992). *The educational annotation of ICD-9-CM* (4th ed., Vols. 1-3). Reno, NV: Channel.

Rabow, J., Schwartz, C., Stevens, S., & Watts, R. (1982). Social psychological dimensions of alcohol availability. *International Journal of the Addictions, 17,* 1259-1271.

Reuter, P. (1992). The limits and consequences of U.S. foreign drug control efforts. *The annals of the American Academy of Political and Social Science, 521,* 151-162.

Rice, D. P., Kelman, S., Miller, L. S., & Dunmeyer, S. (1990). *The economic costs of alcohol and drug abuse and mental illness: 1985.* San Francisco: University of California, Institute for Health and Aging.

Richman, A. (1985). Human risk factors in alcohol-related crashes. *Journal of Studies on Alcohol,* Supplement No. 10, 21-31.

Ripple, W. J. (Ed.). (1989). *Fundamentals of geographic information systems: A compendium.* Bethesda, MD and Falls Church, VA: American Congress on Surveying and Mapping and American Society for Photogrammetry and Remote Sensing.

Rosenberg, C. E., & Golden, J. (Eds.). (1992). *Framing disease: Studies in cultural history.* New Brunswick, NJ: Rutgers University Press.

Rosenbloom, D., Dawkins, C., & Hingson, R. (1992) *Who is really fighting the war on drugs?* Boston: Boston University.

Ross, H. L. (1982). *Deterring the drinking driver: Legal policy and social control.* Lexington, MA: D.C. Heath.

Rush, B. R., & Gliksman, L. (1986). The distribution of consumption approach to the prevention of alcohol-related damage: An overview of relevant research and current issues. *Advances in Alcohol and Substance Abuse, 5,* 9-32.

Rush, B. R., Gliksman, L., & Brook, R. (1986). Alcohol availability, alcohol consumption and alcohol-related damage. *Journal of Studies on Alcohol, 47,* 1-10.

Saffer, H., & Grossman, M. (1987). Drinking age laws and highway mortality rates: Cause and effect. *Economic Inquiry, 25,* 403-417.

Saltz, R. F., Gruenewald, P. J., & Hennessy, M. (1992). Candidate alcohol problems and implications for measurement: General alcohol problems, outcome measures, instrumentation, and surrogates. In H. D Holder & J. M. Howard (Eds.), *Community prevention trials for alcohol problems: Methodological issues* (pp. 35-56). Westport, CT: Praeger.

Sellin, T. (1931, September). The basis of a crime index. *Journal of Criminal Law and Criminology,* 346.

Sellin, T., & Wolfgang, M. E. (1964). *The measurement of delinquency.* New York: John Wiley.

Sherman, L. W. (1992). Attacking crime: Police and crime control. In M. Tonry & N. Morris (Eds.), *Modern policing* (pp. 159-230). Chicago: University of Chicago Press.

Skinner, H. A., & Allen, B. A. (1982). Alcohol dependence syndrome: Measurement and validation. *Journal of Abnormal Psychology, 91,* 199-207.

Smart, R. A. (1980). Availability and the prevention of alcohol-related problems. In T. C. Harford, D. A. Parker, & L. Light (Eds.), *Normative approaches to the prevention of alcohol abuse and alcoholism* (pp. 123-146). Washington, DC: Government Printing Office.

Smith, E. A., & Winterhalder, B. (1992). *Evolutionary ecology and human behavior.* New York: Aldine de Gruyter.

Stoneall, L. (1983). *Country life, city life: Five theories of community.* New York: Praeger Scientific.

Terleckyj, N. E., & Coleman, C. D. (1992a). *Regional economic growth in the United States: Projections for 1992-2010* (Vol. 1; Regional Economic Projection Series Report No. 91-R-1). Washington, DC: NPA Data Services.

Terleckyj, N. E., & Coleman, C. D. (1992b). *Regional economic growth in the United States: Projections for 1992-2010* (Vol. 3; Regional Economic Projection Series Report No. 91-R-3). Washington, DC: NPA Data Services.

Treno, A. J., Cooper, K., & Roeper, P. (1994). Estimating alcohol involvement in trauma patients: The search for a surrogate. *Alcoholism: Clinical and Experimental Research, 18,* 1306-1311.

Treno, A. J., Nephew, T. M., Ponicki, W. R., & Gruenewald, P. J. (1993). Alcohol beverage price spectra: Opportunities for substitution. *Alcoholism: Clinical and Experimental Research, 17,* 675-680.

Treno, A. J., Parker, R. N., & Holder, H. D. (1993). Understanding U.S. alcohol consumption with social and economic factors: A multivariate time series analysis, 1950-1986. *Journal of Studies on Alcohol, 54,* 146-156.

Tuma, N. B., & Hannan, M. T. (1984). *Social dynamics: Models and methods.* New York: Academic.

United Nations. (1989). *Handbook on social indicators.* New York: Department of International Economic and Social Affairs, Statistical Office.

Wagenaar, A. C. (1986a). Preventing highway crashes by raising the legal minimum age for drinking: The Michigan experience six years later. *Journal of Safety Research, 17*(3), 101-109.

Wagenaar, A. C. (1986b). The legal minimum drinking age in Texas: Effects of an increase from 18 to 19. *Journal of Safety Research, 17*(4), 165-178.

Wagenaar, A. C., & Holder, H. D. (1991). Effects of alcoholic beverage server liability on traffic crash injuries. *Alcoholism: Clinical and Experimental Research, 15,* 942-947.

Wagenaar, A. C., & Streff, F. M. (1989). Macroeconomic conditions and alcohol impaired driving. *Journal of Studies on Alcohol, 50,* 217-225.

Warren, R. L. (1983). A community model. In R. M. Kramer & H. Specht (Eds.), *Readings in community organization practice (3rd ed., pp. 27-42).* Englewood Cliffs, NJ: Prentice Hall.

Watts, R. K., & Rabow, J. (1983). Alcohol availability and alcohol-related problems in 213 California cities. *Alcoholism: Clinical and Experimental Research, 7*(1), 47-58.

Williams, G. C. (1992). *Natural selection: Domains, levels, and challenges.* New York: Oxford University Press.

Williams, G., Grant, B., Stinson, F., Zobeck, T., Aitken, S., & Noble, J. (1988). Trends in alcohol related morbidity and mortality. *Public Health Reports, 103,* 592-597.

Wonnacott, R. J., & Wonnacott, T. H. (1979). *Econometrics* (2nd ed.). New York: John Wiley.

Zador, P. L., Lund, A. K., Fields, M., & Weinberg, K. (1988). *Fatal crash involvement and laws against alcohol-impaired driving.* Washington, DC: Insurance Institute for Highway Safety.

Index

About the Authors

Paul J. Gruenewald is Psychologist and Senior Research Scientist at the Prevention Research Center of the Pacific Institute for Research and Evaluation in Berkeley, California. He has served as Principal Investigator on National Institute on Alcohol Abuse and Alcoholism (NIAAA) funded studies that have focused on the combined use of archival and survey research in the evaluation of state and local community systems. He is currently Director of Survey Research Services at Prevention Research Center, Director of the Health Services Prevention Research Post Doctoral Training program funded by NIAAA, Principal Investigator on an NIAAA-funded study of forms and distributions of alcohol availability, and Director of the Alcohol Access Component of the Community Trials Project, also funded by NIAAA. He has published studies examining the role of drinking patterns in drinking problems, the relationships of alcohol price and availability to use, cirrhosis mortality, suicide, traffic crashes and drunk driving, and the application of geostatistical models to community evaluation studies.

Michael D. Klitzner is Principal Social Scientist at the CDM Group, Inc., in Chevy Chase, Maryland. He has received research grants and contracts from the National Institute on Drug Abuse, the National Institute on Alcohol Abuse and Alcoholism, the National Highway Traffic Safety Administration, the Robert Wood Johnson Foundation, and the Medical Trust of the Pew Memorial Trusts. His publications address drug prevention, early intervention, and treatment, impaired driving, primary care approaches to drug and alcohol misuse, research methods, and health policy. He has served as a consultant to the Pan American Health Organization, the American Medical Association, the United States Department of Education, and the National Institutes of Drug Abuse and Alcoholism Abuse. His current research interests focus on the application of systems theory to health systems analysis and health policy development and the impact of managed care on health service delivery.

Gail Taff received a Master's degree in Public Health from the University of California, Berkeley in 1986. She has worked on research and evaluation projects at the federal, state, and local community levels, on topics as diverse as primary care needs and nutrition education program development. Her major area of interest is the relationship between behavior and health, primarily as regards the health effects of nutrition and substance use and abuse. Ms. Taff is a board member of the California Public Health Association—North.

Andrew J. Treno is Sociologist and Research Scientist at the Prevention Research Center of the Pacific Institute for Research and Evaluation in Berkeley, California. He is currently evaluating media advocacy and community mobilization for the Community Trials Project, funded by the National Institute on Alcohol Abuse and Alcoholism. He is also Principal Investigator on the Alcohol Availability and Injury Project, funded by the Alcoholic Beverage Medical Research Foundation. He has published in the areas of alcohol consumption patterns, alcohol availability, media advocacy and community organization evaluation, and alcohol-involved injuries.